Robert Whitford is a retired civil servant who spent most of his career working on overseas health projects on behalf of the Northern Ireland government. In the course of this work, many interesting and amusing situations arose and these are recorded in his first book, *Born in the USSR*, published in 2018.

In the late 1980s, just before embarking on this international career, he took the decision to invest in a holiday property in Castelnaud-de-Gratecambe in South West France. It was a good decision as the apartment was an ideal place in which to chill out between difficult and challenging overseas missions. It has also been the location for many eventful holidays over the intervening years. Lighter moments from those years are captured in the author's second book, *That's your Lot (& Garonne)*, published in February 2020.

Both books have been re-published on Amazon in 2021 along with the author's third book, *The Days of our Lives*, which tells the full story of his life.

Throughout his career, Robert Whitford has had many and varied contacts with the institutions of the European Union. These have included: a short secondment to UKREP in

Brussels, negotiations in the committees of the European Council leading to a special EU agricultural support programme for the Less Favoured Areas in Northern Ireland and the implementation of a number of international health development programmes under contracts with the European Commission. As a result of these contacts, the author has developed an understanding and appreciation of the European Union and the positive impact its institutions have had on many aspects of life at home and abroad.

Consequently, in common with most of his fellow-countrymen in Northern Ireland, he has been deeply affected by the outcome of the 2016 referendum and the resultant departure of the UK from the European Union. Developments since the referendum have provoked a line of thought that has resulted in the story of *The Flight of the Gaels*.

To my son, Michael, and daughter-in-law, Alison, and those of my family and friends who share my European identity.

Robert Whitford

The Flight of the Gaels

A story of the break-up of
the United Kingdom

AUSTIN MACAULEY PUBLISHERS™

LONDON · CAMBRIDGE · NEW YORK · SHARJAH

A CIP catalogue record for this title is available from the British Library.

ISBN 9781398452329 (Paperback)
ISBN 9781398452336 (ePub e-book)

www.austinmacauley.com

First Published 2022
Austin Macauley Publishers Ltd®
1 Canada Square
Canary Wharf
London
E14 5AA

There are many people with whom I have interacted on European matters over the past 50 years. These have included European Commission officials in different directorates, delegates at European Council meetings, staff members at UKREP (the UK Permanent Representation to the European Union), development aid counterparts in Europe and Asia, colleagues working on EU-funded projects and friends and colleagues at home and abroad with whom I have shared thoughts on Europe on many occasions.

As might be expected, views on Europe encountered in most of these settings have been very positive, given the central role of the EU in the working lives of those concerned. Only in the latter setting (interaction with friends and colleagues) has a greater range of views been encountered. For example, in the Leprechauns' golf society of which I am a member at Clandeboye Golf Club in Northern Ireland, views range from apoplectic Europhobia to strong Europhilia.

Perhaps more surprisingly, a similar range of views exists amongst those UK citizens who live in or choose to spend significant amounts of time in the part of SW France we visit each summer. Intuitively, it might be assumed that in all cases such Francophiles would also be Europhiles. In fact, a significant minority amongst this group hold Europhobic views, a phenomenon I have difficulty in understanding.

I am happy to acknowledge that all of these points of view have played into the thought processes that have led to the storyline of *The Flight of the Gaels*.

Table of Contents

Preface   11

Abbreviations   13

Chapter 1: The Answer Is 'We're Out!'   14

Chapter 2: The Aftermath   26

Chapter 3: Hogmanay 2018/2019   37

Chapter 4: The 2019 Tory Civil War   45

Chapter 5: The 2019 Tory Civil War (Part 2)   56

Chapter 6: Brainstorming in Leuven   65

Chapter 7: 2020 – A Virulent Year   73

Chapter 8: The Gaelic Alliance   105

Chapter 9: Referendum Year, 2022   127

Chapter 10: The Gaelic Federation   148

Chapter 11: The Death Throes of Brexit   159

Preface

The timeframe for this book is the nine years from 2016, the year of the Brexit referendum, to 2025. The first five years are set against a background of actual developments whilst the remainder is an imagined view of how things might turn out given the various prevailing winds in the different countries of the United Kingdom.

In the view of the author, the twists and turns that have delivered us to where we are in the year 2021, have combined to create a perfect storm.

Elements of the perfect storm have included: the disarray in the Conservative party which led David Cameron to his ill-fated decision to hold an in-out referendum; the flawed prospectus for the referendum which denied votes to the young, to British expatriates in Europe and to Europeans in the UK, all groups that were likely to vote Remain; the designation of the referendum as advisory, thereby removing the requirement for a threshold higher than a simple majority and the subsequent decision to regard the result as binding; the failure to properly deal with overspending by the Leave campaign or to control digital manipulation and interference in the referendum process by internet bots and the failure of the Labour Party to provide effective opposition.

The prevailing winds that have informed the author's imagined view of the next five years include; ever-hardening English nationalism which shows scant regard for the impact of the Brexit project on other countries of the UK; Boris Johnson's resistance to a second independence referendum, which is fuelling Scottish nationalism; the rise of Sinn Fein in the Republic of Ireland and the growing support in Northern Ireland for a border poll and the early drawing of red lines by Boris Johnson's government which resulted in the hardest of Brexits at the end of 2020.

The names of the central characters (John Campbell, Angus Crawford, Sean Donnelly, Mary Douglas, Jane Harrington, Jim Kearney, Maeve McDermott and Niall Murphy) are fictitious. Those of other characters featuring in the factual backdrop are real, even if the events surrounding them in the period after October 2021 are imagined.

Abbreviations

CA: Cambridge Analytica

Coreper: Committee of Permanent Representatives

DUP: Democratic Unionist Party

EC: European Commission

ECJ: European Court of Justice

ERG: European Research Group

EU: European Union

GA: Gaelic Alliance

GAP: Gaelic Alliance Party

GF: Gaelic Federation

GDP: Gross Domestic Product

MEP: Member of the European Parliament

NHS: National Health Service

SCA: Special Committee on Agriculture

SDLP: Social Democratic & Labour Party

SNP: Scottish National Party

TD: Teachta Dála (Irish MP)

UUP: Ulster Unionist Party

UKRep: UK Permanent Representation to the European Union

Chapter 1
The Answer Is 'We're Out!'

It was Jim Kearney's turn so the venue was Room 46 in the UKREP building on Rond Point Schuman, just across from the Berlaymont Building, Brussels headquarters of the European Commission. The date was 24 June 2016 and the tipple was Black Bush. Jim and his two mates, Angus Crawford and Niall Murphy, had the habit of meeting up around 6.00pm every Friday evening to chew over the developments of the past week and to put the world to rights.

Jim and Angus, from Belfast and Edinburgh respectively, were First Secretaries with UKREP (UK Permanent Representation to the European Union) and Niall, from Dublin, held an equivalent position with the Irish Permanent Representation. All were in their early 30s. The friends took it in turn to host the get-togethers and would provide liquid refreshment appropriate to their country of origin – Bushmills whiskey for Jim, Bells whisky for Angus and Jamieson for Niall.

The mood was sombre at the 24 June get-together. The shock result of the referendum was still sinking in, with David Dimbleby's words "…the British people have spoken and the answer is *we're out!*" still ringing in their ears. After a few tots, the mood began to lighten however, and the rationalisation began.

Niall reckoned things weren't that bad. After all, Ireland had held several referendums on EU issues, with both the Treaty of Nice and the Treaty of Lisbon being rejected by the electorate, before subsequently being approved in second votes. The justification for this had been that people weren't really properly informed when they voted against the treaties. Given the serious consequences for Ireland if the rejection was allowed to stand, it seemed reasonable to launch an information campaign and then allow the electorate to make a more-informed decision.

The Brexit referendum had been advisory so there was no compunction on Government or Parliament to accept the outcome. Given that the result was pretty tight and given the far-reaching consequences for the country, surely some consideration would be given to launching an information campaign and running a second referendum.

Angus wasn't so sure. The UK had never really bought into the flexible attitude to European affairs, adopted by most member states, preferring to play everything by the book.

This British attitude of unwavering correctness was a matter of great puzzlement to the French in particular. Jim recalled an episode of the BBC programme Dateline London in which Gavin Esler had put to the panel of European newspaper correspondents the dilemma faced by the government of the day in relation to a proposed ban on fox hunting. How could the views of the mainly urban anti-hunting lobby and those of country dwellers who wished to continue with their sport be reconciled.

The correspondent from *Le Monde* couldn't see the problem and opined that the matter could be easily resolved – by simply enacting legislation banning fox hunting, thereby satisfying the anti-hunting brigade, and then not bothering to enforce it, satisfying the pro-hunting side! When the laughter had subsided, Gavin Esler suggested that this approach probably wouldn't work in the UK.

Niall felt that on something as fundamental as EU membership, a bit more important than fox hunting, the Government would surely want to take action that would be in the best interests of the country – basically to save people from themselves. At the very least, they would probably go for a soft Brexit, staying within the single market and the customs union. It could be argued that this would be a reasonable approach given the closeness of the result.

The chat then turned to the issues that seemed to have driven the negative attitude to the EU. Chief amongst these was the idea that a 'bunch of unelected bureaucrats' was in control of the affairs of the European Union; hence the perceived need to 'take back control'. Unfortunately, over the years, no attempt had been made to explain the democratic structures of the EU. The 'unelected bureaucrats' were civil servants – just like the unelected bureaucrats in the UK civil service. Neither civil service was responsible for taking decisions – in both cases, decisions were taken at political level and were entirely democratic.

There was an elaborate EU decision-making process with member states having multiple opportunities to influence outcomes. The European Commission was responsible for making proposals. Council working groups, made up of representatives of each member state, would then consider these proposals. Jim, Angus and Niall knew the system well as it was one of their key responsibilities to attend these working groups and to defend the interests of their countries during the discussions. When the working groups had advanced matters as far as they could, issues would then be referred up to the next level – SCA, the Special Committee on Agriculture, in the case of agriculture and fisheries and Coreper, the Committee of Permanent Representatives, for all other sectors. Permanent Representatives based in Brussels and senior civil servants from the member states would take discussions a stage further in these meetings before the Council of Ministers (comprising relevant ministers from each member state) would take the final decisions. What could be more democratic?

The discussion then turned to other matters and it was decided to return to the Brexit issue as and when developments began to unfold. Sir Ivan Rogers, the UK Permanent Representative was due to speak to UKREP staff the following Monday about the referendum result and some interesting points were likely to emerge, given Sir Ivan's close involvement in the developments leading up to the referendum.

Jim and Angus were due to return to the UK in a few days' time for post-referendum briefing in their home departments – they had been seconded to UKREP from the Northern Ireland Department of Agriculture and the Scottish Economy Directorate respectively. The next Friday get together wouldn't be until 15 July and there would be plenty to discuss by then. As well as Sir Ivan's briefing meeting and the briefing sessions in Northern Ireland and Scotland, there would be feedback from Niall who had undertaken to take soundings with colleagues in the European Commission about how they saw things unfolding.

*****

The Irish Permanent Representation to the EU is located on Rue Froissart, a five-minute walk from the UKREP building. Niall had set up three glasses of Jamieson ready to fuel the continuing Brexit discussions on the evening of 15 July.

First to kick off was Angus who, as well as attending briefing sessions with the Scottish Government, had taken advantage of his time in Edinburgh to take soundings among friends and colleagues about attitudes to the unfolding Brexit drama. Having heard from Sir Ivan Rogers on 27 June that his continuing advice to Ministers in London was to move in the direction of a deal that would minimise economic disruption, he had been shocked to hear the early pronouncements from Theresa May, recently crowned successor to David Cameron. Her assertion that 'Brexit means Brexit' and her appointment of Brexiteers to key positions in her new government, including the appointment of Boris Johnson as Foreign Secretary, seemed to suggest that the direction of travel would be far from that recommended by Sir Ivan.

The attitude of the Scottish Government and of people in Scotland in general was one of disbelief that a narrow and flawed victory for the 'No' campaign was being interpreted as a mandate for a hard Brexit. This was particularly galling for Scotland, given that the country had voted to remain in the EU and had done so by a margin that was a lot bigger than the English margin for leaving. Many people were of the opinion that the referendum should have required a leave majority in all four constituent countries of the UK rather than allowing the most populous of the four countries to force the others out against their wills.

A strong view was emerging that a further referendum on Scottish independence would be justified, given that the situation had changed so dramatically since 2014. Unionists had always maintained that the 2014 vote had been a once-in-a-generation event but they had also argued at the time that a vote to remain in the UK was a vote to remain in the EU and that if Scotland became independent, there was no guarantee that the new state would be admitted to the EU. Now the situation had been turned on its head – remaining in the UK was a sure way for Scotland to **leave** the EU!

The official briefings Angus had attended had focussed on the problems Scotland would suffer as a result of Brexit – particularly a hard Brexit which seemed to be a likely outcome if the Europhobes in the Tory party were to be allowed to continue calling the tune. Chief amongst these problems would be the impact of an end to freedom of movement. Scotland's demography was such that there would be a growing demand for workers from EU countries to fill key positions in a wide variety of sectors including social services, health, agriculture and the hospitality sector. At the very least, special arrangements would have to be made to protect Scottish interests.

Feedback from Jim on his time back in Northern Ireland touched on many of the same points. Like Scotland, Northern Ireland had voted to remain in the EU by a significant margin. Inexplicably, the Democratic Unionist Party, the main pro-union party in Northern Ireland, had supported Brexit and had even channelled a £0.5 million donation to support the Leave campaign in Great Britain. It seemed likely that they had done this in the mistaken belief that Brexit would result in a hardening of the Irish border, something that would be very appealing to their voter base. What they had failed to appreciate was that, due to the international commitments enshrined in the Good Friday Agreement, such a hardening of the border could not be allowed to happen. The need to maintain an open Irish border would, in the event of a hard Brexit, lead inevitably to some sort of border between Northern Ireland and Great Britain – hardly a welcome outcome for staunch unionists!

Jim's antennae had picked up that something of a rear-guard action might already be under way in that plans were afoot for Arlene Foster, First Minister and Leader of the DUP, and Martin McGuinness of Sinn Fein, Deputy First Minister, to send a joint letter to Theresa May, calling for special measures to protect Northern Ireland interests. Clearly, the best way to protect those interests would have been for the DUP to oppose Brexit, in line with all the other political parties in Northern Ireland.

As regards the specific threats posed by Brexit, those identified in Scotland had also been flagged up in Northern Ireland, especially the threat that would be posed by ending freedom of movement. The border was an even bigger issue however as, apart from security issues, any kind of trade restriction would cause significant disruption to the agrifood sector with its dependence on multiple trade flows back and forward across the frontier.

As in the case of Scotland, the fishing industry had supported Brexit on the assumption that the UK would be able to keep EU boats out of British waters resulting in a bigger share of the available fish for local fishermen. The fish-processing sector was less sanguine, fearing that a *quid pro quo* for keeping EU boats out of British waters could be a closing off of the European markets – the main outlet for British fish and fish products.

While the others had been sussing out attitudes in Scotland and Northern Ireland, Niall had been networking with friends and colleagues in the European institutions to find out how the EU was likely to handle the negotiations for the UK's withdrawal. The first reaction he had encountered was one of disbelief that the 'No' campaign had triumphed. David Cameron had been advised by several key Europeans, including Donald Tusk, President of the European Council and a number of senior Eurocrats not to take the risk of an in-out referendum. They were all too aware of the negative publicity against the EU that had been a feature of the British right-wing press since the day and hour of the UK's accession. Brussels-based correspondents for the right wing press had misrepresented what was happening in Europe and had peddled a lot of misinformation including the suggestion that Brussels intended to ban the sale of bent bananas!

Little attempt to counter this often inaccurate and hysterical campaign had been made by successive British governments because of the parties' fear of provoking negative coverage from the right-wing press with resultant damage to their electoral prospects. Commission officials also acknowledged that they should have done more to promote the positive benefits of EU membership over the years. In this connection, there should have been a much bigger promotional role for the network of EU delegations in member countries. Negative attitudes had been allowed to fester, largely unchallenged, for decades and it was probably not surprising that the 'remain' side had been unable to turn these attitudes around in the short timeframe of the referendum campaign.

The Commission was already turning its attention to the process that would have to be followed to facilitate the UK's disengagement. There would have to be a Withdrawal Agreement before any trade talks could begin and the elements that would need to be included in this agreement were beginning to emerge. They would include a financial settlement; arrangements for protecting EU citizens in the UK and UK citizens in the EU, and arrangements to ensure continued free movement of goods, services and people across the Irish border.

Work had started on putting together an EU negotiating team for the Brexit talks and Michel Barnier, former EU Commissioner and French Foreign Minister, seemed to be the front runner to take on the role of Chief Brexit Negotiator. A trawl would soon be launched to fill other posts in the negotiating team and it had been put to Niall that he might like to put his name forward for one of the positions. Niall's period of secondment to the Irish Permanent Representation was due to come to an end in December 2016 and it would be an option for him to consider applying to the Commission, rather than returning to the Irish Department of Foreign Affairs in Dublin. Given the central importance of the Irish border in the forthcoming negotiations, the Irish Government would undoubtedly welcome the involvement of one of its officials on the Brexit negotiating team.

With the August holidays just around the corner, the three drinking companions vowed to continue their close interest in Brexit affairs in the coming weeks and to meet up again in September when there would no doubt be many more twists and turns to mull over. Jim's and Angus's periods of secondment would continue for a further 9 and 15 months respectively so there would still be a base for the Friday meetings. In the event that Niall succeeded in getting a post in the Commission's Brexit negotiating team, it was agreed that the aim would be to keep the little group of Europhiles together. They would do what they could to influence things in a sensible direction in the coming months.

The shocking news on the morning of 24 June 2016

Rond Point Schuman, Brussels, with the Berlaymont building (HQ of the European Commission) on the left and the UKREP (UK 'Permanent' Representation) building far centre

Theresa May speaks to reporters, shortly after being elected leader of the Conservative Party

Michel Barnier, front-runner to take on the role of EU Chief Brexit
negotiator
(Creative Commons Attribution 2.0 Generic (CC-BY-20))

Chapter 2
The Aftermath

As expected, on 27 July, Michel Barnier, was named Chief EU Negotiator for the imminent Brexit talks on the UK's withdrawal terms. Two weeks later, Niall Murphy received confirmation that his application for a post with the Brexit negotiating team had been successful. With the August holidays approaching, nothing much would be happening until the autumn so Niall bade farewell to his colleagues in the Irish Representation and headed for Dublin and a welcome summer break.

Over the summer period, the recriminations continued in the UK over various aspects of the referendum process – regarded as deeply flawed by many commentators. It also became clear that the 'Leave' side had been caught off-guard by its unexpected success. Most surprising of all was the emerging realisation that no plan existed for implementing the result of the referendum. Despite this fact, Theresa May announced to the Conservative Party conference on 2 October that she would trigger the EU's Article 50 (the mechanism to set the formal exit process in motion) by the end of March 2017. To the dismay of EU leaders (and remain voters in the UK), her speech set out a number of unhelpful red lines and included a pledge to make the UK a 'fully independent sovereign country'. It was clear that the advice she had been receiving from UKREP about protecting the UK economy by remaining close to the EU customs union and single market, had fallen on deaf ears.

One month later, the UK High Court ruled that the Government could not trigger Article 50 without parliamentary approval, a decision later confirmed by the Supreme Court. True to form, the Daily Mail condemned the judges who had made the ruling as 'enemies of the people'. The remainder of the right-wing press joined in blaming the legal profession for trying to 'frustrate the will of the British people'.

Around this time, it became clear that the 'will of the people' had in fact been seriously manipulated, thanks to the activities of the political consulting firm, Cambridge Analytica (CA). Links between CA and Facebook were exposed by a former CA employee, Christopher Wylie. He revealed that data from millions of people had been shared without their permission. Using this data, pro-Brexit messages had been sent to large numbers of voters, making it more likely that they would vote Leave in the referendum.

Wylie also showed that a Canadian business with links to Cambridge Analytica's parent company had carried out research for the Vote leave campaign in the lead up to the 2016 referendum. This research was likely to have breached the UK's laws on campaign financing and to have helped sway the outcome of the referendum,

He also revealed that Vote Leave had been working with BeLeave, a campaign group aimed at young Brexiteers. A couple of BeLeave whistleblowers told Parliament that Vote Leave had been directing their activities. Combining campaigns in this way is illegal under UK law, as is the combining of campaign finances. The two organisations, along with the DUP, were accused of working together illegally in the period leading up to the referendum.

Despite all of these revelations and despite a further uncompromising speech by the Prime Minister at Lancaster House, Parliament did give its approval to the initiation of the leave process and, on 29 March 2017, Theresa May sent a letter to European Council President Donald Tusk, triggering Article 50. The letter set the date for the UK's departure from the European Union as 29 March 2019.

By early April, Jim Kearney had completed his period of secondment to UKREP and returned to the Northern Ireland civil service. Fortunately for him, a competition was launched soon after his return, to fill two vacant Assistant Secretary positions and Jim was successful in securing one of them. The post, in the Office of the First and Deputy First Ministers, put him at the heart of government and would give him a bird's eye view of the developing drama surrounding Brexit – or so he thought! Unfortunately, there had already been a dramatic development three months earlier – the collapse of the power-sharing government at Stormont, brought on by a scandal surrounding a renewable heat initiative. By the time Jim took up the post, its future was already in some doubt.

Meanwhile, back at Westminster, Teresa May decided that in order to secure the uncompromising Brexit she was seeking, she would need to bolster her majority in Parliament. On 18 April, she announced a snap general election, despite having insisted on multiple occasions that she had no intention of doing so. It was a bad miscalculation as the Conservatives lost their majority at the June poll and were forced to do a deal with the DUP to stay in power.

Some weeks earlier, the European Commission (mandated by the European Council) had published its key negotiating issues for the forthcoming talks on the UK's withdrawal. Niall Murphy's earlier prediction as to what these issues would be, turned out to be correct – the UK's divorce bill, citizens' rights and arrangements for the Irish border would be central to the process.

With the talks about to get underway, our three Europhile friends were now in very strategic positions, Angus Crawford still had six months to do at UKREP, Jim Kearney was at the centre of political developments in Northern Ireland – a key battleground for Brexit – and Niall Murphy was on Michel Barnier's Brexit negotiating team. Their get-togethers were about to get a lot more interesting, even if the logistics of their meetings would be more difficult.

Talks on the UK withdrawal got under way in mid-July and signs of a more realistic British attitude soon began to emerge. During a speech in Florence, despite advice to the contrary from the right wing European Research Group, Theresa May gave notice that the UK would honour its budget commitments. She proposed a post-Brexit transition period, during which the UK would for two years continue to follow EU rules and pay into the EU budget. The transition period would be used to agree details of the EU / UK trading arrangements that would apply post-Brexit.

In early December a joint EU / UK report was published indicating significant progress on the main withdrawal issues and the prospect that talks could move in the New Year to consider future trading relationships.

*****

Jim Kearney had now been in his new post for eight months and hadn't really settled. The absence of a functioning devolved government meant that many of the potentially more interesting aspects of the job were missing and he wondered how long it would be before the post was suppressed. In early December, an advertisement had appeared in the Belfast Telegraph and had caught his attention. It was for a 2-year research fellowship leading to a Master's degree at Ulster University, focusing on the constitutional impact of Brexit. Certain guidelines were laid down but the precise design of the research project was left to be proposed by interested applicants. The successful applicant would be the one who submitted the most innovative and relevant project proposal, in the eyes of the adjudicators. Jim decided to have a go and set about preparing his application. In the event that he was successful, he would apply for a 2-year career break from the Civil Service.

Angus Crawford had just returned to the Scottish Economy Directorate, having completed his period of secondment to UKREP. Jim got in touch to tell Angus about his proposed career change and to arrange a get together. He was keen to develop a research proposal that was as widely based as possible and was hoping that, with Angus's help, he might be able to design a project that would look at the implications of Brexit for both remain-leaning parts of the UK.

With Christmas approaching, they decided to wait till January for their meeting. The plan was for Jim to join Angus in Edinburgh for the 2017 / 2018 New Year celebrations and, once the hangovers had disappeared, to get down to business.

*****

The talks stretched over three days, with a research plan beginning to emerge by the end of the second day. Under the plan, focus group discussions would be held with a range of different interest groups in Scotland and Northern Ireland. The issues emerging from the focus groups would be used to frame a number of questions for inclusion in a Delphi survey which would again be implemented in both countries.

The Delphi method is a structured communication technique, originally developed as an interactive forecasting method which relies on a panel of experts. The method is based on the principle that forecasts, or decisions, from a structured group of individuals are likely to be more accurate than those from unstructured groups. The respondents answer questionnaires individually in two or more rounds. After each round, a facilitator or change expert provides an anonymised summary of the responses from the previous round. In this way, respondents are encouraged to revise their earlier answers in light of the replies of other members of their panel (the identity of those other members being unknown to them). The idea is that during this process, the range of the answers will decrease and the group will converge towards the 'correct' answer. The process is brought to a halt after a predefined stop criterion such as number of rounds, achievement of consensus or stability of results.

First applications of the Delphi method were in the field of science and technology forecasting but later the method was applied in other areas, especially those related to public policy issues, such as economic trends, health and education. It had also been used as a tool to implement multi-stakeholder approaches for policy making in developing countries.

Jim and Angus were convinced that an interesting research proposal could be developed in the area of post-Brexit decision making in Remain-voting areas, using the Delphi methodology. The closing date for applications for the Ulster University research fellowship was still some weeks away so Jim had plenty of time after his return to Belfast to develop the idea and get an application pulled together.

The application was submitted in early February and Jim was notified two weeks later that his proposal had been short-listed along with three others. The short-listed applicants were invited to make oral presentations on their proposals in the first week of March and Jim was notified soon after that he had been successful. He would be able to begin his research in October.

*****

Meanwhile, the Brexit saga itself continued to unfold. Further hints of compromise were given in a speech by

Theresa May at the Mansion House in London. Significant UK concessions were emerging in key policy areas such as the role of the European Court of Justice (ECJ), freedom of movement, budget contributions and fishing rights.

In March, a draft EU / UK agreement on the UK's withdrawal was published. However, many sections of the report were highlighted to show that agreement had yet to be reached.

Four months later, Theresa May's much-trumpeted 'Chequers Plan' was presented to the cabinet. The plan, named after the prime minister's country residence where it had been discussed, was an elaboration of her earlier policy of managed divergence from EU rules. The tone of the document pointed to a significantly softer Brexit than had previously been envisaged. Included was the idea of a common rule book on goods moving between the UK and the EU.

Two days after the presentation of the Chequers Plan, May's Brexit minister, David Davis, resigned and foreign secretary, Boris Johnson, followed suit the following day. In due course, a total of 18 ministers resigned in opposition to the Chequers Plan.

At a summit in Salzburg in September, the Prime Minister received a hostile reception from EU leaders over her Plan. It was described as an exercise in cherry-picking from EU rules. EU Council President, Donald Tusk, argued that much of the plan was unworkable and posed a threat to the single market. Michel Barnier was particularly scathing about the proposals relating to the Irish border.

In November, the UK and the EU struck a deal on the UK's exit terms but the deal was torpedoed by Arlene

Foster, Leader of the Democratic Unionist Party. She objected to the draft provisions relating to the Irish border (the Irish border backstop) which would involve Northern Ireland (but not Great Britain) remaining closely aligned to the EU Customs Union and Single Market. Because of the government's reliance on DUP support for its survival, Foster's objections could not be ignored. The deal was tweaked bringing the whole of the UK into the customs union alignment but leaving only Northern Ireland with regulatory alignment. The DUP accepted the revised deal.

Strong opposition to the deal soon began to emerge in the UK parliament. It was clear that many Tory MPs were becoming increasingly restive and that Theresa May's problems were far from over. On 13 December she managed to survive a vote of confidence in her leadership of the Conservative Party but this was achieved on condition that she would step down before the next election. A parliamentary vote on the deal in parliament was delayed till January 2019.

The Guardian reports on Theresa May's disastrous 2017 general
election result

Ulster University, new Belfast campus
(Copyright Albert Bridge: Creative Commons Attribution –
ShareAlike 2.0 Generic (CC-BY-SA-2.0))

Theresa May meets Jean-Claude Junker in Brussels

Chapter 3
Hogmanay 2018/2019

Jim Kearney was able to negotiate his two-year career break from the civil service and had taken up his new position at Ulster University at the beginning of October 2018. He would spend the first few months refining his research proposal in discussion with colleagues at the university and in the community. He was also keen to touch base with Angus Crawford and Niall Murphy before embarking on the field-work element of his research. The friends agreed to meet up in Edinburgh over the new year period, taking in the Hogmanay celebrations before getting down to an exchange of views on Jim's new project.

As an appetiser for their discussions, Niall suggested they should have a competition to highlight the absurdity of the whole Brexit process. He asked Jim to draw up an A to Z of what was wrong with Brexit and Angus to produce an A to Z of the opportunities that Brexit would unlock. He would assess the two efforts and declare a winner during their get together.

The friends assembled in Edinburgh on 29 December and that evening decided to conduct the adjudication at a hostelry close to Angus's apartment, just off Princes Street.

After a few pints, Jim handed round copies of his effort. It read as follows:

The A to Z of What's Wrong with Brexit

A is for Anglo-centric worldview. This is the view of the world that seems to motivate many Brexiteers. It was neatly encapsulated in a London evening newspaper headline from many years ago 'Fog in the Channel – Europe Cut Off'. People with this mindset are uncomfortable with the idea of pooling sovereignty with countries in Europe and yearn for a return to the days of Empire.

B is for Bent Bananas, which, according to the Eurosceptic media, were to be banned by the EU. This was typical of the ridiculous newspaper stories that appeared in the right-wing press over many years, poisoning the attitude to Europe of a large section of the UK public.

C is for Cambridge Analytica and the manipulation of the social media which helped to deliver Brexit; targeting people with fake news to create anti-EU prejudice or strengthen such prejudice where it already existed.

D is for DUP, the party which received 28% of the popular vote in Northern Ireland in 2017 and yet is the only voice in Westminster representing Northern Ireland on Brexit. The DUP uses its close relationship with the Tory party to push for a hard Brexit, against the wishes of Northern Ireland agriculture, business and 56% of Northern Ireland voters who opted for Remain.

E is for Europhobe. Let's drop the term 'Eurosceptic' which implies that someone has their doubts about the European project. Being doubtful suggests that you are weighing up the pros and cons and aren't too sure. There hasn't been much sign of that in the European Research Group! Indeed, there hasn't been much sign of research in the European Research Group either!

F is for Foreign Interference, notably from Russia. Brought to bear largely through social media, this played a part in delivering the Brexit vote. The question is, who has our interests more at heart – Moscow or Brussels?

G is for GDP, set to decline under any of the current Brexit scenarios. It is surely questionable for Parliament to deliver an economic downturn, with associated job losses and reduced living standards, by arguing that it is 'the will of the people'.

H is for Heat versus Light, one of the characteristics of the debate leading up to the Brexit vote. A virtual absence of detailed analysis of the pros and cons meant that people had only a vague idea of what they were voting for.

I is for Ireland, north and south, which is set to suffer significant economic and political damage, in the interests of English nationalism.

J is for Japanese disinvestment. Although Brexiteers are in denial that there is any connection, it is increasingly clear that the prospect of a still-undefined Brexit is driving Japanese and other investment out of the country.

K is for the Knowledge that decisions should be based on – a far cry from the tendency of some Brexiteers to discount the views of experts as metropolitan elitism.

L is for Lies of which many were peddled during the referendum campaign. A notable example was the promised extra £350 million a week for the NHS.

M is for Margin of Victory which amounted to 52%/48% in favour of Brexit. Although frequently referred to as 'a clear victory' it was of course nothing of the sort. An issue of such national constitutional significance ought to require the support of more than 37% of the electorate.

N is for NHS, which is set to suffer significant negative consequences as a result of Brexit. Instead of an extra £350 million a week, the health service is likely to receive reduced funding due to the predicted decline in GDP and rather than providing protection from hordes of EU spongers, Brexit will result in fewer EU nationals being available to deliver NHS services to the UK population.

O is for Overspending of which Vote Leave has been found guilty. For some reason, this does not seem to be regarded as having any significance for the result.

P is for Project Fear. This mantra is trotted out whenever any negative consequences of Brexit are identified. It is very useful for Brexiteers as it eliminates the need for any reasoned counter arguments. Many of the economic warnings from the Remain side (said to have been discredited in the immediate aftermath of the vote) are already turning out to be true, even before the UK's departure.

Q is for the Quagmire in which the UK now finds itself. (Sorry, that's the best I could do for Q).

R is for Referendum No 3 – yes, No 3, not No 2. Those opposed to a People's Vote argue that the vote has already taken place. However, when circumstances change (such as new information or evidence of people changing their minds) a further vote is justified. This is the only way the

2016 referendum (No 2) can be justified, given that we had already had one (No 1) in 1975.

S is for Scottish Independence which, like Irish reunification, is being given a boost by the Brexit process. The potential breakup of the United Kingdom seems to be a price most Brexiteers think is worth paying in order to reach those sunny uplands.

T is for Turkey which, according to the Leave campaign, would unleash tens of millions of migrants to our shores if we did not exit the EU. No sign of them yet.

U is for the Unelected bureaucrats in Brussels, supposedly running our lives in a totally undemocratic way. The European Commission (= civil service) is indeed unelected as is the civil service in the UK. EU decisions on the other hand are taken by elected Ministers (including British ones) just as they are in the UK.

V is for the Voting Parameters adopted for the Brexit referendum. These were flawed in several respects. Most significantly, for a binding referendum, there should have been a threshold of say 40% of the eligible electorate. The way chosen to get around this was to describe the vote as advisory and then, after the event, to regard it as binding – increasingly referred to as the 'instruction of the British people'.

W is for Will of the People. This is another frequently employed mantra but for some reason the Brexiteers accord more importance to the will of the people expressed in 2016, based on minimal information, than to the potential will of the people that would be expressed in a People's vote in 2019, based on voluminous information. Could it be something to do with opinion polls showing a swing in favour of Remain?

X is for the X that would have been placed on the Brexit referendum voting slip in favour of Remain by 16- and 17-year-olds, by EU nationals in the UK and by UK nationals in the EU had they been allowed to vote. 16- and 17-years olds (who were allowed to vote in the Scottish Independence referendum) will have to live with the consequences of Brexit longer than any of those who were allowed to vote.

Y is for the Yawning Gap between what was promised by the Leave campaign and what is now on offer, under any scenario.

Z is for Zilch which appears to be the sum total of the benefits that will be realised from Brexit! (Sorry, that's the best I could do for Z).

When the applause had died down, Angus handed out his sheet of paper. On it was written 'Sorry, I couldn't think of any opportunities that Brexit will unlock'!

Jim was declared the winner.

The Hogmanay celebrations came and went. In the discussions proper, Jim was keen to explore ways in which his research could be supported in Scotland. The mechanics of running the focus groups and Delphi survey in Northern Ireland were fairly clear and he would have plenty of logistical support from Ulster University colleagues. Angus was keen to help but thought it would be difficult for him as a civil servant to get directly involved in the project. However, his sister was a lecturer in politics at the University of St Andrews and Angus was sure Mary wouldn't need too much persuading.

At this stage, Jim wasn't too sure whether or when there would need to be some project activity in the Republic of Ireland. Niall offered to explore options for support in the Republic in the event that this would be needed.

*****

Shortly after his return to Belfast, Jim got a call from Mary Douglas confirming that she would be happy to provide support for extension of the Ulster University project to Scotland. Mary travelled to Belfast the following week to discuss the methodology for the first stage of the project – the running of focus groups to identify key issues for the Delphi surveys. Mary had had experience of running focus groups in a number or earlier projects and was able to help with the process for ensuring that the groups would be as representative of the target populations as possible and with the procedures to follow to ensure that the group discussions would produce reliable results.

The work of establishing and running the focus groups was completed in both jurisdictions by the first week of February and questionnaires for the first round of the Delphi survey were ready to issue two weeks later.

Hogmanay celebrations in Edinburgh, 2018/2019
(Creative Commons Attribution 2.0 Generic)

Reaction to Brexit of border communities in Ireland

Chapter 4
The 2019 Tory Civil War

Back in the world of UK politics, the civil war which had been brewing in the Conservative Party broke out in earnest from the start of 2019. In parliament, on 15 January, the government lost the first 'meaningful vote' on the Brexit deal by 432 votes to 202, the worst parliamentary defeat in the history of the United Kingdom.

Two weeks later Theresa May was given a mandate by MPs to return to Brussels to renegotiate the Irish backstop arrangements. This she did and at the beginning of February the renegotiated deal was presented to parliament. It was defeated by 149 votes, this in light of the attorney-general's conclusion that there was no guarantee that the revised deal would allow the UK to pull out of the backstop unilaterally.

On 20 March, at the behest of parliament, the Prime Minister asked the EU to delay Brexit by three months to 30 June. The EU's response was to offer two alternative extensions – to 12 April if the deal failed or to 22 May if it was passed.

A few days later several hundred thousand pro-EU protesters marched in London in support of a further referendum on the UK's EU membership.

At the end of March the government lost a third parliamentary vote on the Brexit deal by a margin of 58 votes. Significantly, MPs were also unable to reach agreement on any alternative solution, including the idea of a second referendum.

*****

Work on the Delphi survey had meanwhile been proceeding during March, with panels of respondents being selected in each of 11 local authority areas in Northern Ireland and 31 local authority areas in Scotland. Each panel consisted of 45 individuals selected to ensure a representative spread of both genders, all age groups and a variety of political affiliations.

The questionnaire was issued to all the respondents at the end of March with a deadline for return by 15 April. Questionnaires for Northern Ireland respondents were administered by Jim Kearney from his base at the Jordanstown campus of Ulster University while those for Scottish respondents were administered by Mary Douglas from her base at St Andrews University.

A key feature of the Delphi survey methodology is that respondents are unknown to each other. The questionnaires were to be completed by each individual without reference to others on the panels. Only those administering the survey would have an overall view of the responses, allowing them to focus in on apparent areas of converging consensus.

Jim and Mary spent the second half of April collating the returns and coming up with average scores for the response to each of the round 1 questions. These scores would not be communicated to the respondents but would be used by the survey teams to develop a new set of questions for round 2 of the survey.

DELPHI SURVEY ROUND 1 – RESULTS

1. WHICH OF THE FOLLOWING POST-BREXIT ISSUES WORRIES YOU MOST (RANK IN ORDER OF IMPORTANCE TO YOU):
(i) THE ENDING OF 'FREEDOM OF MOVEMENT'; <u>3</u>
(ii) DISRUPTION AT BORDERS; <u>5</u>
(iii) WITHDRAWAL OF THE EUROPEAN HEALTH INSURANCE CARD (EHIC) BENEFITS; <u>6</u>
(iv) REDUCED OPPORTUNITIES FOR STUDY IN EUROPE; <u>8</u>
(v) IMPACT ON PRICE AND AVAILABILITY OF MEDICINES; <u>2</u>
(vi) RE-INTRODUCTION OF ROAMING CHARGES WHEN IN EU COUNTRIES; <u>9</u>
(vii) REDUCED COORDINATION OF ACTION AGAINST CRIME AND TERRORISM; <u>4</u>
(viii) REDUCTION IN LIVING STANDARDS DUE TO PREDICTED FALL IN GDP; <u>1</u>
(ix) REDUCED NEGOTIATING POWER FOR TRADE DEALS; <u>10</u>
(x) REDUCED STANDARDS FOR PRODUCE COMING FROM NON-EU COUNTRIES? <u>7</u>
IF YOU ARE NOT WORRIED ABOUT ANY OF THESE ISSUES, PLEASE EXPLAIN WHY. <u>0 RETURN</u>

---

2. **IN RELATION TO ENDING FREEDOM OF MOVEMENT, WHICH OF THE FOLLOWING STATEMENTS DO YOU BELIEVE TO BE TRUE?**

(i) IT SHOULD REDUCE THE PRESSURE ON PUBLIC SERVICES. <u>11%</u>

(ii) IT WILL RESULT IN SKILLS SHORTAGES IN KEY AREAS. <u>88%</u>

(iii) IT SHOULD IMPROVE COMMUNITY COHESIVENESS. <u>1%</u>

3. **IN RELATION TO DISRUPTION AT BORDERS, WHICH OF THE FOLLOWING WORRIES YOU MOST (RANK IN ORDER OF IMPORTANCE):**

(i) LONG QUEUES AT PASSPORT CONTROL; <u>NI 4, SCOTLAND 1</u>

(ii) DISINVESTMENT/LOSS OF JOBS DUE TO INTERRUPTION OF JUST-IN-TIME' SUPPLY LINES; <u>NI 3, SCOTLAND 2</u>

(iii) NEW TIME-CONSUMING PROCEDURES FOR MOVEMENT OF GOODS BETWEEN GREAT BRITAIN AND NORTHERN IRELAND; <u>NI 2</u>

(iv) PRICE INCREASES DUE TO TARIFFS ON GOODS ENTERING NORTHERN IRELAND FROM GREAT BRITAIN? <u>NI 1</u>

4. DO YOU EXPECT TO BE PERSONALLY DISADVANTAGED BY NOT HAVING A EUROPEAN HEALTH INSURANCE CARD? <u>68% YES</u> IF NOT, WHY? <u>32% NO – HAVE NEVER USED ONE</u>

5. DO YOU EXPECT TO BE PERSONALLY DISADVANTAGED BY REDUCED OPPORTUNITIES FOR STUDY IN EUROPE? <u>34% YES</u> IF SO, WHY? <u>FAMILY MEMBERS' PLANS AFFECTED</u>

6. WHICH OF THE FOLLOWING STATEMENTS BEST DESCRIBES YOUR ATTITUDE TO THE POST-BREXIT POLITICAL SITUATION?

(i) WE SHOULD ACCEPT THAT WE HAVE LEFT THE EUROPEAN UNION AND PUT THE CONTROVERSY SURROUNDING THE 2016 REFERENDUM BEHIND US. **26%**

(ii) REMAIN-VOTING COUNTRIES OF THE UK SHOULD FIND A WAY TO RE-CONNECT WITH THE EUROPEAN UNION. **74%**

7. IF YOU ANSWERED (II) TO QUESTION 6, WHICH OF THE FOLLOWING STRATEGIES WOULD YOU SUPPORT?

(i) WORK WITHIN THE EXISTING POLITICAL SYSTEM IN THE UK TO BUILD SUPPORT FOR A FUTURE REFERENDUM ON RE-JOINING THE EU. **38%**

(ii) CAMPAIGN FOR A BORDER POLL AND RE-ENTRY TO THE EU, THROUGH THE CREATION OF A UNITED IRELAND (NORTHERN IRISH RESPONDENTS). **27%**

(iii) CAMPAIGN FOR A FURTHER INDEPENDENCE REFERENDUM LEADING TO SCOTTISH INDEPENDENCE AND SCOTTISH MEMBERSHIP OF THE EUROPEAN UNION (SCOTTISH RESPONDENTS). **35%**

8. IF YOU SELECTED STRATEGY 7 (II), WHICH IF ANY OF THE FOLLOWING GIVE YOU CAUSE FOR CONCERN?

(i) THE STANDARD OF LIVING IN THE NEW IRELAND; 32%

(ii) HEALTH AND SOCIAL SERVICE STANDARDS IN THE NEW IRELAND; 36%

(iii) PENSION ISSUES IN THE NEW IRELAND; 38%

(iv) CIVIL UNREST AMONGST THOSE OPPOSED TO THE UNIFICATION OF IRELAND. 41%

9. IF YOU SELECTED STRATEGY 7 (III), WHICH IF ANY OF THE FOLLOWING GIVE YOU CAUSE FOR CONCERN?

(i) THE STANDARD OF LIVING IN THE NEW SCOTLAND; 36%

(ii) HEALTH AND SOCIAL SERVICE STANDARDS IN THE NEW SCOTLAND; 34%

(iii) PENSION ISSUES IN THE NEW SCOTLAND; 35%

(iv) CURRENCY ISSUES IN THE NEW SCOTLAND; 43%

(v) CROSS-BORDER DISRUPTION BETWEEN SCOTLAND AND ENGLAND; 41%

With civil war continuing in the Tory party, it was clear that the Brexit deadline would have to be extended yet again. At a special summit in early April EU leaders approved an extension of the UK's membership until the end of October. The deal was a flexible one, allowing the UK to leave the EU earlier, if the Withdrawal Bill was passed in good time.

Because of the protracted delays caused by the turmoil in parliament, the UK would still be a member of the EU on 23 May, the date of the European Parliamentary elections. The country would therefore be obliged to take part in the elections. This further weakened Theresa May's position and she was forced to agree to stand down as Tory leader by 27 June. She would remain as prime minister pending the election of a new leader.

The European election results were catastrophic for both the Tories and the opposition Labour Party. Nigel Farage's Brexit Party performed strongly as did the pro-remain parties. Arguably, the election results represented a victory for Remain as the combined vote of the remain-leaning parties exceeded that for leave-leaning parties.

This outcome was assisted by the strong performance of remain candidates in both Scotland and Northern Ireland. In both countries the size of the remain majority increased over that recorded at the 2016 referendum. Northern Ireland's three MEPs were now split 2 remain/1 leave versus the 1 remain/2 leave that pertained before the election. This swing was due largely to the strong performance of the Alliance Party's Naomi Long, a development which also had implications for Northern Ireland politics as only one of the three MEPs was now from the loyalist tradition.

*****

While this drama was being played out, Jim Kearney and Mary Douglas were working hard on their analysis of the round 1 Delphi results in Northern Ireland and Scotland and the design of the questionnaire for round 2.

The most significant of the responses related to question 7, focussing on the constitutional future of the two countries. The combination of votes for working within the existing political system to build support for a future referendum on re-joining the EU and campaigning for a border poll in Ireland amounted to 66%. The combination of votes for working for a new referendum on re-joining the EU and campaigning for a second Scottish independence referendum was even more convincing at 75%.

The responses to questions 8 and 9, dealing with causes for concern amongst those supporting an Irish border poll and a second independence referendum respectively, showed that the 66% and 75% combined vote figures might be a bit fragile. It would be necessary to tease out these causes for concern to explore in what ways the concerns might be mitigated.

Two other groups requiring deeper investigation were the people who wanted to move on from the referendum (might there be developments that would encourage them to move from this position in the direction of seeking a means of re-connecting with the EU?) and the people who wanted to find an unspecified means of re-connecting with the EU (might there be developments that would encourage them to move from this general pro-EU position to the more specific pro-EU position of supporting a border poll or a second independence referendum?).

The design for the Delphi round 2 questionnaire emerged from these deliberations. The responses had been gathered in by the beginning of July.

DELPHI SURVEY ROUND 2 – RESULTS

1. IN ROUND 1, WHICH OF THE FOLLOWING STATEMENTS DID YOU SELECT AS BEST DESCRIBING YOUR ATTITUDE TO THE POST-BREXIT SITUATION?

(i) WE SHOULD ACCEPT THAT WE HAVE LEFT THE EUROPEAN UNION AND PUT THE CONTROVERSY SURROUNDING THE 2016 REFERENDUM BEHIND US. <u>26%</u>

(ii) REMAIN-VOTING COUNTRIES OF THE UK SHOULD FIND A WAY TO RE-CONNECT WITH THE EUROPEAN UNION. <u>74%</u>

2. IF YOU SELECTED OPTION (I), WHICH OF THE FOLLOWING DEVELOPMENTS MIGHT PERSUADE YOU TO SWITCH YOUR SUPPORT TO OPTION (II)?

(i) EVIDENCE EMERGING THAT THE UK WILL BE WORSE OFF OUTSIDE THE EU. <u>51%</u>

(ii) EVIDENCE EMERGING THAT PRO-EU SENTIMENT IS INCREASING WITHIN PARLIAMENT. <u>39%</u>

3. FOR NI RESPONDENTS: IF, IN ROUND 1, YOU SELECTED OPTION 6 (II) (REPRODUCED AT 1 (II) ABOVE) AND OPTION 7 (I) (WORK WITHIN THE EXISTING POLITICAL SYSTEM…), WHICH OF THE FOLLOWING DEVELOPMENTS (IN ORDER OF PRIORITY) MIGHT PERSUADE YOU TO SWITCH YOUR SUPPORT TO OPTION 7 (II) (CAMPAIGN FOR A BORDER POLL…)?

(i) EVIDENCE OF IMPROVED LIVING STANDARDS IN THE REPUBLIC OF IRELAND. <u>3</u>

(ii) UNDERTAKINGS ABOUT THE QUALITY AND AFFORDABILITY OF HEALTH AND SOCIAL CARE IN THE NEW IRELAND. <u>2</u>

(iii) GUARANTEES THAT PENSIONS EARNED IN THE UK WOULD BE PROTECTED IN THE NEW IRELAND. <u>2</u>

(iv) EVIDENCE OF BUY-IN TO ANY NEW CONSTITUTIONAL ARRANGEMENT BY BOTH COMMUNITIES IN NORTHERN IRELAND. <u>1</u>

4. **FOR SCOTTISH RESPONDENTS: IF, IN ROUND 1, YOU SELECTED OPTION 6 (II) (REPRODUCED AT 1 (II) ABOVE) AND OPTION 7 (I) (WORK WITHIN THE EXISTING POLITICAL SYSTEM…), WHICH OF THE FOLLOWING DEVELOPMENTS (IN ORDER OF PRIORITY) MIGHT PERSUADE YOU TO SWITCH YOUR SUPPORT TO OPTION 7 (III) (CAMPAIGN FOR A FURTHER INDEPENDENCE REFERENDUM…)?**

(i) A CONVINCING STRATEGY FOR MAINTAINING LIVING STANDARDS AFTER INDEPENDENCE. <u>1</u>

(ii) A CONVINCING STRATEGY FOR ENSURING THE QUALITY AND AFFORDABILITY OF HEALTH AND SOCIAL CARE AFTER INDEPENDENCE. <u>3</u>

(iii) GUARANTEES THAT PENSIONS EARNED IN THE UK WOULD BE PROTECTED AFTER INDEPENDENCE. <u>2</u>

(iv) A SATISFACTORY DECISION ON THE CURRENCY TO BE USED AFTER INDEPENDENCE. <u>2</u>

(v) CLARITY ON THE REGIME TO APPLY TO MOVEMENTS OF GOODS AND PEOPLE ACROSS THE SCOTLAND/ENGLAND BORDER. <u>4</u>

London Pro-EU parade on 25 March 2019

European Parliament: one of the regular announcements on turnout
and result projections for the 2019 European Parliamentary
election

Chapter 5
The 2019 Tory Civil War (Part 2)

True to her word, Theresa May stepped down from the Tory Party leadership on 7 June and the six-week campaign to identify her successor began. From the outset, Boris Johnson emerged as the clear front-runner, despite the numerous gaffs and shortcomings that many felt had defined his party career since completing his time as London Mayor. For the anti-EU party faithful, his uncompromising support for Brexit was all that mattered.

After several weeks of ballots, Johnson did indeed emerge as the clear winner, defeating Jeremy Hunt, the other surviving candidate, by margin of 2 to 1. On the 24 July, he moved into Downing Street as the UK's new prime minister.

There was a widely held view that once Johnson had secured the leadership he would soften his approach and move in the direction of a sensible Brexit. This couldn't have been further from the truth and from day one the rhetoric was stepped up. Every utterance seemed to point more and more strongly to the likelihood of a no-deal departure from the European Union. Soon after taking office, the new prime minister issued a formal request to the EU to ditch the Irish backstop from the withdrawal agreement. The EU immediately refused and the scene was set for a bloody confrontation in the months ahead.

*****

As the political situation continued to deteriorate, Jim Kearney and Mary Douglas were hard at work analysing the results of round 2 of the Delphi survey.

The first interesting development they noted was that those who had earlier indicated a hard-line position of accepting the referendum result and moving on, were now acknowledging that in certain circumstances, they might be ready to soften their view. In particular, they might make such a move if evidence was to emerge that the UK would be worse off outside the EU.

There were also indications that those who had earlier opted for a general position of seeking to re-align with the EU, might now be prepared to move in the direction of more specific action to achieve this outcome. In the case of Northern Ireland, evidence of buy-in to any new constitutional arrangement by both communities and undertakings on health care and pensions would be likely to shift respondents in the direction of supporting a border poll. In the case of Scotland, a convincing strategy for maintaining living standards after independence, guarantees on pensions and a satisfactory decision on the currency to be used after independence would be likely to shift respondents in the direction of supporting a further independence referendum.

In light of these shifts in position, Jim and Mary set about developing the questionnaire for the third round of the

Delphi process, focusing more closely on the narrowing options that seemed likely to command a consensus at the end of the process.

*****

Back at Westminster, things were not improving. The UK Parliament was prorogued for five weeks on advice given to the Queen by Boris Johnson's government. This move was strongly supported by the Eurosceptic wing of the Tory party but on 3 September, 21 pro-Europe Conservative MPs voted against the government in protest at the prorogation and its strategy of driving the UK towards a 31 October exit from the EU with or without an agreed deal. The 21 rebels were unceremoniously expelled from the party.

Soon after this momentous decision, Boris Johnson ramped up the rhetoric even further by declaring that he would rather 'die in the ditch' than ask for another Brexit extension. There would be several similar statements over the summer and early autumn pointing to the inevitability that the UK would leave the EU by 31 October, come what may.

The pro-Europe wing of the party wasn't taking this lying down and on 9 September, they helped a bill promoted by the veteran labour MP, Tony Benn to become law, preventing the UK from leaving the EU on a no-deal basis, without parliament's consent. Two weeks later, the Supreme Court ruled that the government's suspension of parliament had been unlawful and, consequently, the Houses of Parliament reopened for business.

The drift towards a more and more extreme position continued and the Conservative Party conference opened on 29 September with a newly-coined slogan 'Get Brexit Done'. This slogan dominated the airwaves in the following weeks in much the same way that 'Take Back Control' had during the referendum campaign. The UK was becoming a cold house for those with a European identity.

On 3 October, Johnson's government sent a new Brexit plan to Brussels, a central plank of which was the removal of the Irish backstop. The government's resolve had no doubt been strengthened by an opinion poll amongst Conservative party supporters which had shown that these patriots regarded achievement of a pure Brexit as more important than maintaining the integrity of the United Kingdom. They would happily see Northern Ireland and Scotland leaving the fold, provided they could achieve their Brexit goal.

Needless to say, Johnson's new Brexit plan was greeted with great scepticism and was roundly rejected by the European Commission three days after it was received.

*****

By the middle of September, responses to the Delphi survey third round questionnaire had been received and made for interesting reading.

DELPHI SURVEY ROUND 3 - RESULTS

1. WHICH OF THE FOLLOWING STATEMENTS BEST DESCRIBES YOUR ATTITUDE TO IRISH UNITY OR SCOTTISH INDEPENDENCE?

(i) I AM IMPLACABLY OPPOSED. <u>41%</u>

(ii) I AM UNDECIDED BUT COULD BE PERSUADED IF CERTAIN RESERVATIONS COULD BE DEALT WITH SATISFACTORILY. <u>35%</u>

(iii) I AM FULLY BEHIND THE IDEA. <u>24%</u>

2. IF YOU OPTED FOR STATEMENT (II), TO WHAT EXTENT WOULD THE FOLLOWING CIRCUMSTANCES CONTRIBUTE TO REMOVING YOUR RESERVATIONS? (ALLOCATE A PERCENTAGE FOR EACH WITH THE FOUR PERCENTAGES TOTALLING NO MORE THAN 100%).

FOR NI RESPONDENTS

(i) THE UK GOVERNMENT AGREES TO UNDERWRITE THE COST OF PENSIONS EARNED IN THE UK FOR RESIDENTS OF THE NEW IRELAND COMING FROM NORTHERN IRELAND. <u>22%</u>

(ii) THE UK GOVERNMENT AGREES TO UNDERWRITE THE ADDITIONAL COSTS ASSOCIATED WITH CONVERTING THE EXISTING HEALTH CARE SYSTEM IN THE IRISH REPUBLIC TO AN NHS-TYPE SYSTEM FOR THE NEW IRELAND. <u>20%</u>

(iii) THE REPUBLIC OF IRELAND CONTINUES TO OUT-PERFORM THE UNITED KINGDOM IN THE AREA OF ECONOMIC GROWTH. <u>23%</u>

(iv) AN IMAGINATIVE SOLUTION IS FOUND WHICH ENSURES SUPPORT FOR THE NEW IRELAND FROM BOTH SIDES OF THE COMMUNITY DIVIDE IN NORTHERN IRELAND. <u>35%</u>

FOR SCOTTISH RESPONDENTS

(i) THE EU WELCOMES SCOTLAND'S APPLICATION FOR MEMBERSHIP AND OFFERS A PACKAGE OF SUPPORT TO CUSHION THE IMPACT OF SEPARATION FROM THE UK (INCLUDING THE IMPACT OF TRADE BARRIERS ON THE BORDER WITH THE UK). <u>35%</u>

(ii) THIS PACKAGE IS DEPENDENT ON SCOTLAND BECOMING A MEMBER OF THE EURO-ZONE. <u>10%</u>

(iii) THE UK GOVERNMENT AGREES TO UNDERWRITE THE COST OF PENSIONS EARNED IN THE UK FOR RESIDENTS OF AN INDEPENDENT SCOTLAND. <u>25%</u>

(iv) ECONOMIC MODELLING SUGGESTS THAT GDP IN AN INDEPENDENT SCOTLAND WITHIN THE EU WILL GROW FASTER THAN IN THE UK. <u>25%</u>

It was clear from these responses that, as a means of preserving their European identity, respondents might be ready to support Irish unity and Scottish independence, provided certain conditions could be met. In both countries, these conditions were mainly of an economic nature, to do with pensions, health services and relative GDP growth levels, although in Northern Ireland the potential for inter-community conflict was also an important factor.

Jim and Mary concluded that one more survey round would probably be sufficient to achieve the optimum possible level of consensus. It could be useful at this stage to re-involve Angus Crawford and Niall Murphy before finalising the round 4 questionnaire.

*****

Following the rejection by the Commission of the British government's new Brexit plan, a further round of UK-EU talks got under way in Brussels and, not surprisingly, collapsed in acrimony. EU Council President, Donald Tusk, accused Johnson of playing a 'stupid blame game'.

An unexpected development took place however on 10 October when Boris Johnson met the Irish Taoiseach, Leo Varadkar, at the Thornton Manor Hotel on the Wirral, Cheshire. A 'pathway to a possible deal' emerged from the talks and this led to the EU and UK agreeing to intensify negotiations. A week later, in advance of a scheduled Brussels summit, it was announced that a new Brexit deal had been agreed. The deal would involve the UK in particular making major concessions over Northern Ireland.

The compromise involved Northern Ireland only, rather than the whole of the UK, remaining closely aligned with the EU Customs Union. As had been the case with Theresa May's deal, Northern Ireland would also remain closely aligned with the EU Single Market. Effectively, Northern Ireland would remain within the European Union. Although hailed as a great achievement by Johnson, this new deal on Northern Ireland was exactly the same as the original one proposed by the Commission but rejected by Theresa May.

At a special Saturday sitting of parliament on 19 October, MPs in the House of Commons withheld their approval for the deal until laws implementing Brexit were in place. This meant that Boris Johnson would be obliged to ask the EU for another Brexit delay. The pressure on the beleaguered prime minister was ramping up and this was intensified further by another huge 'People's Vote' pro-EU march in central London.

Three days later, Boris Johnson put the Brexit legislation, designed to implement his deal with the EU, on hold, stating that he had no alternative due to obstruction by Brexit-denying pro-EU MPs.

On 28 October, the EU agreed to offer the UK a Brexit 'flextension' until 31 January 2020. Parliament formally approved this offer the next day and one day later approved a 12 December general election. Boris Johnson had already asked for a general election on numerous occasions but now he had finally got his way.

The remain-leaning parliament had failed to get its act together and had handed Johnson his chance to deliver a hard Brexit, against the wishes of an emerging majority in the country. In the preceding months, a number of opinion polls had pointed to a shift away from the narrow pro-Brexit referendum vote towards a majority in favour of remain.

On 12 December, the UK general election was won convincingly by the Conservatives who gained an 80-seat majority. Needless to say, Scotland and Northern Ireland registered strong anti-Brexit majorities.

There was now nothing to stop the Eurosceptic Tories from delivering the hardest of Brexits.

Protests outside Downing Street against the prorogation of
Parliament
(Copyright Julian Osley: Creative Commons Attribution –
ShareAlike 2.0 Generic (CC-BY-SA-2.0))

The media await the Supreme Court ruling on the
prorogation
(Copyright Steve Nimmons: Creative Commons Attribution 2.0
Generic (CC-BY-2.0))

Chapter 6
Brainstorming in Leuven

Jim's research project had reached the stage of designing the fourth and final round of the Delphi survey. He had been ably assisted by Mary Douglas in designing and implementing the first three rounds but he felt that it would be useful to involve the other members of their original brainstorming group – Angus Crawford and Niall Murphy – in the final stage of the process. Christmas was approaching and the thought occurred to him that a repeat of the previous year's Hogmanay get together might provide the right environment for creative thinking.

Niall was still working on Michel Barnier's Brexit team but he would have a couple of weeks off around Christmas and New Year. He didn't intend to return to Dublin however as he was planning to spend the holiday with his new French girlfriend, Sylvie. His suggestion was that the get together should take place in Belgium rather than Scotland. He had some good connections with the Irish College at Leuven, 20 km east of Brussels, and was sure he would be able to organise some rooms for the group.

The Irish College was established in 1984 as an international residential centre with a mission to promote understanding of and opportunities for the island of Ireland through: provision of education and training programmes for higher education institutions, business organisations, public sector bodies and voluntary and community associations; the hosting of lectures, colloquia, seminars, conferences and workshops; and the facilitation in continental Europe of all forms of cultural expression from the island of Ireland.

The others agreed that this sounded like an ideal location for the brainstorming session and Niall was deputed to organise four double rooms (Jim, Angus and Mary would bring their spouses) and a meeting room at the college for the period running from 30 December 2019 to 4 January 2020. The plan was to enjoy the New Year celebrations in Brussels and get down to business on the Delphi concluding questionnaire once their heads had cleared.

The group duly met up in a small conference room on the ground floor of the college on the morning of 2 January. Jim Kearney chaired the session and began by drawing attention to the finding that 60% of respondents in round 3 (combined Northern Ireland and Scottish respondents) had indicated some level of support for Irish Unity or Scottish independence. However, less than half of these were fully behind the idea. The remainder would need to have a number of reservations dealt with before they could embrace the significant constitutional change involved in leaving the UK.

A number of anticipated reservations had been identified in the third-round questionnaire and Jim suggested they might proceed by looking at each of these in turn, starting with the most significant reservations as indicated by the level of importance attached to each by the respondents.

The highest scoring reservation (mentioned by 35% of Scottish respondents) related to the impact of separation from the UK on the Scottish economy, including the impact of trade barriers on the border with England. How could this issue be dealt with in the round 4 questionnaire so as to give some level of reassurance? The experience of the Irish Republic in dealing with the aftermath of the 2008 financial crash might give some cause for optimism. Despite the serious economic downturn in the Republic, the country had managed within 10 years to recover to a point where the economy was growing again at a rate in excess of 5% of GDP. This had been due in no small measure to the support made available to Ireland by the EU. Contrary to received wisdom at the time, membership of the Eurozone had not acted like a millstone around the neck of the country but had been part of the support mechanism leading to its recovery.

Ireland's experience might help to reassure Scottish voters that any economic disruption arising from independence would be mitigated by support that would probably be forthcoming from the EU.

30% of respondents from Northern Ireland cited worries about the health service in a New Ireland and anticipated loyalist opposition to Irish unity as their two biggest reservations. There could be merit in carrying out some research into different health care systems in Europe and their costs compared to the existing UK and Irish systems, neither of which could be described as perfect. Any new service would not necessarily have to replicate the existing NHS system but might be closer to the successful French insurance-based model.

Dealing with likely opposition to constitutional change from the loyalist community would be more problematical and, for the moment, the brainstorming group could not come up with any easy answers.

The issue of pensions had been flagged up by 25% of Scottish respondents and 20% of Northern Ireland respondents. The group thought there were good prospects for the British government being prepared to pick up the bill for pensions earned by civil servants and other public sector workers while they were still British citizens. This was a similar issue to the one affecting British citizens working for the EU institutions before Brexit. The cost of pensions earned by these British Eurocrats was one of the elements making up the UK's Brexit divorce bill. It would be difficult for the government to acknowledge its liabilities in one case and shirk them in the other.

The group was struggling with the question of how best to present these reservations and associated assurances in the round 4 questionnaire when Jim Kearney delivered a curved ball. How would it be if an additional constitutional option was to be included in the final questionnaire? As well as respondents having to choose between the status quo, Scottish independence and Irish unity, why not include a fourth option – the idea of a federation of Ireland and Scotland, within the European Union?

A hush descended followed by loud cheers from the rest of the group. It was now late in the day and Jim was concerned that the euphoria was as much a sign of tiredness and relief that somebody had come up with an idea as anything else. It often happens in such circumstances that the idea loses a lot of its appeal when revisited with a clear mind the next day. So they decided to call it a day and reconvene in the morning. After an excellent meal in a local restaurant, followed by a few digestives, it was time for a good night's sleep.

The meeting the next day got going around 10.00am and began with a suggestion from Jim that somebody else should take over the chair as the main business was to discuss his revolutionary idea and he was probably too close to it to provide objective chairmanship. Once a position had been taken on Jim's idea, the meeting would move to consider the format and scope of the final round Delphi questionnaire. Niall agreed to take the chair.

Nobody had lost enthusiasm for the federation idea overnight and Niall proposed that they should proceed by looking again at the various reservations that were holding respondents back from whole-hearted support for constitutional change. He had already been thinking about this and felt that Jim's proposal might well deal effectively with most of the issues they had talked about the previous day.

It was possible, for example, that Scottish respondents who were nervous about the prospects for an independent Scottish economy would be reassured if their journey was to be taken in tandem with a country whose economy was already performing strongly. Similarly, their worries about adopting the euro might be assuaged by the fact that their new federal partner had already been using the currency successfully for many years.

There was of course a new circumstance to be factored in – the economic impact of a potentially hard border between Scotland and England. Niall pointed out that there had been examples in the past of special packages of measures designed to ease the accession of new members to the EU. He would be happy to speak to colleagues in the Commission to see what they thought about the prospects for such a package to deal with short-term disruption to trade flows that might arise for the proposed new federation.

Such a package might also include an undertaking to protect the pensions of Scottish and Northern Irish public servants, in the event that the British government refused to accept liability for these. Niall felt that this was a bit of a long shot but, in any case, such a refusal was only likely in the event of an acrimonious divorce.

In Niall's view, one of the strongest arguments for the federation idea lay in the reassurance it could provide for Northern Ireland's loyalist community. The two main threats posed to this community by the idea of a united Ireland were: the threat to their British identity; and the perceived danger of becoming a protestant minority in a majority catholic country. The concept of British identity had already been dealt a damaging blow by the revelation that English Tories valued Brexit ahead of continuing links with Northern Ireland, and, of course, the UK country to which loyalists were most strongly attached was Scotland – the country which was likely to leave the UK anyway and with which they could now ensure a continuing link through the proposed federation.

The second reassurance would arise from the demography of the new federation. Scotland with its protestant majority plus Northern Ireland with its roughly 50/50 split and Ireland with its catholic majority would result in a federation with a non-threatening balance of the two religions. The federation would have a total population of 11.85 million, of which 5.37 million would be catholic, and 6.48 million combined protestant and other denominations.

Jim was happy with the reaction to his innovative suggestion and now introduced another innovative idea. Why not locate the federal parliament of the proposed Gaelic Federation at Parliament Buildings in Belfast? With the Irish Parliament based at Leinster House, Dublin and the new Scottish Parliament at Holyrood, Edinburgh, Stormont would be strategically placed to take on the federal role. The others reacted positively and gave this idea the thumbs up.

The discussion then turned to the logistics of the final round survey and a new issue soon cropped up. If the idea of a federation was to be included, the survey would need to be run in the Irish Republic as well as in Northern Ireland. Niall reckoned there wouldn't be a problem with this and agreed to explore prospects for identifying a research partner in one of the Irish universities. A Delphi panel could be established in each of the 26 counties of the Republic and the same questionnaire could be run north and south with the options being the status quo, a united Ireland or a united Ireland as part of an Irish-Scottish Federation. Respondents in Scotland could choose between the status quo, an independent Scotland or an independent Scotland as part of a Scottish-Irish Federation.

The group parted company the next morning in high spirits and agreed to keep in touch as the Brexit drama continued to unfold. Jim was happy that he now had a solid basis on which to move to the final stage of his research project.

Grand Place Brussels – perfect for seeing in the New Year
(Creative Commons Attribution 2.0 Generic (CC-BY-2.0))

The Irish College, Leuven, Belgium
(Creative Commons Attribution – ShareAlike 2.0 Generic (CC-BY-SA-2.0))

Chapter 7
2020 – A Virulent Year

With his thumping majority from the December election, Boris Johnson was never going to have a problem getting his EU Withdrawal Bill through parliament. On 23 January, the bill became law after a passage through parliament that was smooth in the extreme, compared to the havoc of 2019. Six days later, the European Parliament approved the Brexit divorce deal. Accordingly, the UK left the EU officially at midnight, Central European Time, on 31 January 2020.

An 11-month transition period began on 1 February, running to 31 December 2020. During this period, most UK-EU arrangements would remain the same and the UK would continue to pay into the EU budget. Apart from the Brexit-obsessed British government, nobody believed that this would allow sufficient time to sort out the future EU-UK trading relationship.

In the early weeks of 2020, Boris Johnson was asked by the media on several occasions whether he would consider extending the transition period beyond 31 December 2020, if that would be necessary to finalise a sensible trade deal. A request for such an extension would need to be lodged with the EU by July. On each occasion, he responded with an emphatic 'no', claiming that there was plenty of time to agree the deal by the end of the year. Most commentators disagreed, arguing that the time was far too short. What nobody knew at that stage was that the limited time that was available would be needed to deal with a much bigger crisis.

*****

That crisis had its origins some weeks earlier in the city of Wuhan in the People's Republic of China. The Chinese Centre for Disease Control and Prevention published an article in January 2020 reporting that a number of patients with pneumonia of unknown origin had been identified on 21 December 2019. A short time later, a new virus was identified which had infected dozens of people. The Chinese government contacted WHO and agreed to accept an international scientific team to help with their efforts to determine the origins of the virus.

China reported the first death from the virus – identified as a new corona virus – on 11 January. Later in the month, the first confirmed cases outside China occurred in Japan, South Korea and Thailand. Around the same time, the first confirmed case of the virus in the United States was reported in the state of Washington. The man concerned had developed symptoms on his return from a trip to Wuhan. The risk level to the British public from the new virus was increased from 'very low' to 'low' on 22 January.

The Chinese authorities moved to isolate the city of Wuhan on 23 January, prohibiting planes, trains, buses and ferries from leaving the city. Unfortunately, some 100,000 people had already departed from Wuhan Train Station before the shutdown

At this stage, seventeen people had died and 570 had been infected in Taiwan, Japan, Thailand, South Korea and the USA. .

*****

Some weeks earlier, following the Leuven brainstorming session, Niall Murphy had done some serious networking with colleagues in the European Commission. The reaction to the Gaelic Federation concept was unanimously positive and the general feeling was that the EU would want to do as much as possible to facilitate this idea, should the people of Ireland and Scotland eventually vote for it. Brexit had had a very destabilising effect on the Union and, with populist movements on the rise in several member states, the danger of further withdrawal movements developing was very real. A positive move in the opposite direction, such as the accession to the EU of a Gaelic Federation, would be extremely welcome. It seemed likely that a fairly generous accession package might be negotiable, depending on the circumstances at the time.

Niall had also been charged with identifying a research partner in the Republic of Ireland to work with Jim Kearney on the extension of the round 4 Delphi Survey south of the border. A one-week trip back to Ireland gave him the opportunity to sound out contacts at Trinity College, Dublin and at the three campuses of the National University of Ireland. All showed interest but a decision was finally taken in favour of University College, Galway. Sean Donnelly, an old school friend of Niall's was working in the College of Arts, Social Sciences and Celtic Studies at the Galway campus and was very enthusiastic about participating in the project.

Meanwhile, Jim Kearney had been working on the questionnaires for the final round survey. There would be two versions of the questionnaire – one to be administered in Scotland and one in Ireland, north and south. In each case, a set of assumptions would be listed, followed by three options from which respondents would select one:

→ status quo
→ Scottish Independence/Irish unity
→ Scottish independence/Irish unity, within the context of a Gaelic Federation

The questionnaires were issued to the Delphi panels in all three jurisdictions at the end of January.

*****

Also at the end of January, the UK recorded its first two positive cases of the new Coronavirus infection when two Chinese nationals became ill while staying at a hotel in York. When a plane carrying British evacuees from Wuhan arrived at RAF Brize Norton, the passengers were immediately transferred to a specialist hospital on Merseyside to begin 14 days quarantine.

On 30 January, with thousands of new cases occurring daily in China, WHO declared a global health emergency. By this time, 213 people had died and 9,800 were infected worldwide. The UK advised its citizens to leave China unless their presence there was essential.

A week later, Dr Li Wenliang, a young Chinese doctor who had tried to sound a warning about the new infection died after contracting the virus. He had earlier been criticised by the Chinese government for scaremongering and made to sign a statement describing his warning as an unfounded rumour.

On 11 February, the disease caused by the new corona virus was given the official name Covid-19 (standing, for coronavirus disease 2019). By this time, a total of 1,113 people had died in China and 44,653 were infected.

Continuing its relentless spread, the virus next appeared in Iran and South Korea and on 23 February, Italy became the first country in the EU to experience a major spike of cases. The Italian authorities locked down 10 towns in Lombardy after a cluster of cases appeared in Codogno, near Milan. Schools had to close and sports and entertainment events were cancelled. Fifty thousand people experienced the first lockdown in Europe as the Italian government tried to control the spread of the virus.

Cases of the virus surged in the UK in early March and, junior health minister, Nadine Dorries, became the first British MP to test positive for the virus. The US banned travel from European countries other than the UK and Ireland and WHO classified the virus as a pandemic leading to big falls in world stock markets. The UK Chancellor of the Exchequer announced a £12bn package of emergency measures to support the UK economy. Many sporting events were postponed, including the London Marathon and Premier League football fixtures.

By mid-March, the British government had begun daily press briefings in which everyone in the UK was encouraged to work from home. People were also asked to avoid pubs and restaurants to help cut down spread and give the NHS time to cope with the pandemic. Officially, the death toll in the UK had risen to 55, with 1,543 people infected, although unofficial estimates were suggesting a total of 10,000 infections.

On 17 March, the EU banned travellers from third countries from entering the EU although an exception was made for the United Kingdom in view of its transitional relationship. Also on 17 March, France imposed a country-wide lockdown, banning all gatherings and only allowing people to leave their homes for fresh air and exercise. By this time, France had around 6,500 infections and more than 140 people had been killed by the virus.

In the following days, Rishi Sunak, the UK Chancellor of the Exchequer, announced a £350bn package of emergency state support for business claimed to be the biggest since the 2008 financial crash. The package consisted of £330bn of government-backed loans and more than £20bn in tax cuts and grants for companies threatened with closure. The closure of schools across the country from 20 March until further notice was also announced. as was the closure of all pubs, restaurants, gyms and other social venues. The government announced that it would pick up the bill for a furlough scheme that would pay up to 80% of the wages of workers at risk of being laid off.

On 23 March, a lockdown was introduced in England under which people would only be allowed to leave their homes to buy food, access health care, exercise once a day or to go to work if it was impossible for them to work from home. People were also required to maintain a distance of at least two metres from non-family members. Failure to comply with the new measures would result in the imposition of fines. Similar arrangements were introduced in Scotland, Wales and Northern Ireland and comparable measures were in place in the Republic of Ireland. The worldwide Covid-19 total now stood at 270,000 infections and 11,000 deaths.

By the end of the month, several high-profile individuals had become infected with the virus, including Prince Charles, Health Secretary Matt Hancock, Chief Medical Officer Chris Whitty and Prime Minister Boris Johnson. Of these, Boris Johnson was hit hardest and would end up in intensive care at St Thomas' Hospital, across the River Thames from the Houses of Parliament.

*****

Before the lockdown was introduced, Jim Kearney, Sean Donnelly and Mary Douglas had a chance to meet up and review the responses to the round 4 Delphi survey. Although the direction of travel had been fairly clear from the responses to the earlier rounds of the survey, the three researchers were astonished by the political earthquake foreshadowed by the results of the final round survey:

DELPHI SURVEY ROUND 4 RESULTS (IRELAND)

1. BASED ON THE FOLLOWING ASSUMPTIONS, PLEASE CHOOSE ONE OF THE OPTIONS AT (2) AS YOUR PREFERRED OPTION FOR THE FUTURE CONSTITUTIONAL ARRANGEMENT FOR THE ISLAND OF IRELAND:

→ THE ECONOMY OF THE REPUBLIC OF IRELAND CONTINUES TO OUT-PERFORM THAT OF THE UNITED KINGDOM.

→ SCOTLAND VOTES TO BECOME AN INDEPENDENT COUNTRY WITHIN THE EUROPEAN UNION.

→ THE UNITED KINGDOM GOVERNMENT AGREES TO UNDERWRITE THE COST OF PUBLIC SECTOR PENSIONS FOR RESIDENTS OF NORTHERN IRELAND IN ALL CIRCUMSTANCES.

→ THE EUROPEAN UNION AGREES A SPECIAL ECONOMIC PACKAGE TO EASE ANY RE-ACCESSION OF NORTHERN IRELAND TO THE EU, IN THE EVENT OF A VOTE IN FAVOUR OF IRISH UNITY AND/OR AN IRISH-SCOTTISH FEDERATION.

2. PLEASE TICK ONE BOX TO INDICATE YOUR PREFERRED CONSTITUTIONAL ARRANGEMENT:

○ CONTINUATION OF THE *STATUS QUO.* NI 27% RoI 17%

○ UNION OF NORTHERN IRELAND WITH THE REPUBLIC OF IRELAND IN A NEW IRELAND. NI 24% RoI 38%

○ A UNITED IRELAND LINKED TO AN INDEPENDENT SCOTLAND IN A GAELIC FEDERATION WITHIN THE EUROPEAN UNION. NI 49% RoI 45%

DELPHI SURVEY ROUND 4 RESULTS (SCOTLAND)

1. BASED ON THE FOLLOWING ASSUMPTIONS, PLEASE CHOOSE ONE OF THE OPTIONS AT (2) AS YOUR PREFERRED OPTION FOR THE FUTURE CONSTITUTIONAL ARRANGEMENT FOR SCOTLAND:

→ THE ECONOMY OF THE REPUBLIC OF IRELAND CONTINUES TO OUT-PERFORM THAT OF THE UNITED KINGDOM.

→ NORTHERN IRELAND JOINS THE REPUBLIC IN A NEW IRELAND.

→ THE UNITED KINGDOM GOVERNMENT AGREES TO UNDERWRITE THE COST OF PUBLIC SECTOR PENSIONS FOR RESIDENTS OF SCOTLAND IN ALL CIRCUMSTANCES.

→ THE EUROPEAN UNION AGREES A SPECIAL ECONOMIC PACKAGE TO EASE THE ACCESSION OF SCOTLAND TO THE EU EITHER AS A FREE-STANDING COUNTRY OR AS PART OF A SCOTTISH-IRISH FEDERATION.

2. PLEASE TICK ONE BOX TO INDICATE YOUR PREFERRED CONSTITUTIONAL ARRANGEMENT:

○ CONTINUATION OF THE *STATUS QUO*. 26%

○ AN INDEPENDENT SCOTLAND WITHIN THE EUROPEAN UNION. 35%

○ AN INDEPENDENT SCOTLAND AS PART OF A SCOTTISH-IRISH FEDERATION WITHIN THE EUROPEAN UNION. 39%

It was clear from these results that a majority might well exist in both Scotland and Ireland in favour of the idea of a Gaelic Federation within the European Union. This was a dramatic finding from Jim's research and he looked forward to writing it up in the form of a thesis, which he hoped would earn him a Master's degree from Ulster University later in the year. Aside from that, the three research colleagues felt that there would need to be some political follow-up to capitalise on the findings, given their significance. Before they had been able to crystallise their thinking, the lockdown was announced in both Ireland and the UK, so any further deliberations between them would have to be conducted remotely.

In the following days, they exchanged thoughts online and began to hone in on an idea which they thought carried considerable promise, although it would be difficult to put into effect in the circumstances of the lockdown. The idea was to establish a new organisation to be called the Gaelic Alliance. This body would have a presence in Scotland and in both parts of Ireland. Its role would be to lobby in favour of coterminous referenda in Scotland and Ireland, north and south. The Alliance would seek to influence political parties in all three jurisdictions and the UK and Irish governments in favour of such referenda. As and when the polls were agreed, the Alliance would lobby strongly in favour of the Gaelic Federation option.

The logistical task of setting up the new alliance would be impossible to achieve during the Covid-19 lockdown, so the project was put on hold pending developments.

*****

Serious pressures soon began to emerge in the UK in efforts to combat the Covid-19 virus. These included: shortage of ventilators needed to keep the most seriously ill patients alive, and lack of personal protection equipment

(PPE) needed to reduce the risks to front line staff. There were also problems with testing equipment and reagents needed to detect and isolate infected people and facilitate contact-tracing in the community and, most importantly, to clear health care staff enabling them to return to work from isolation.

The government came under serious criticism when it emerged that they may have failed to prepare properly for the pandemic. Many commentators noted that, despite evidence from China in the early stages of Covid-19 pointing to the likelihood that additional medical resources would be required, little attempt had been made to boost stocks of ventilators, PPE or virus testing kits.

The government didn't get around to issuing a call for the production of additional ventilators until mid-March. Evidence then emerged of an apparent government failure in the procurement field. The UK had seemingly chosen not to take part in an EU ventilator procurement exercise under which it could have increased the stock of ventilators for the NHS by aligning with the EU's collective purchasing power.

At first the government said it had decided not to participate because the UK was no longer in the EU. Instead it was 'making its own efforts' to source extra ventilators.

An alternative explanation then emerged – the government had missed the deadline due to a breakdown in communications. This explanation was immediately undermined by the revelation that the UK had received early notice of the joint procurement process and had in fact participated in a number of meetings with the EU at which the process was discussed.

This all pointed to the likelihood that, for ideological reasons, the government had chosen not to take part in an EU initiative to procure life-saving equipment.

Further evidence of apparent incompetence emerged when several ventilator manufacturers reported that they had contacted the government with offers of help but had received no response. One company, had been in touch after sourcing 5,000 ventilators but, in the absence of any interest from the government, had directed the supplies to another country. Another reported that the government had failed to respond to its offers to expand production .

Similar problems were being experienced in relation to supply of PPE. In 2006, according to media reports, the government had spurned expert advice to build up stocks of PPE to prepare for the possibility of an influenza pandemic. This decision had evidently been cost-based and the consequences were now being felt by health service staff who were experiencing serious shortages of equipment at the frontline. Desperate measures were being tried to cope with this situation, including requests to schools to donate science goggles, and decisions by some doctors to acquire and pay for their own protective masks. It seemed likely that UK advice on protective equipment was less robust than that of the World Health Organisation not because they were receiving different advice from different experts but because they needed to preserve limited supplies.

More general issues of under-capacity in the NHS were also exposed by the Covid-19 pandemic. These included a severe shortage of intensive care beds which resulted in the need to cancel all non-urgent elective surgery for a period of around three months. For many years, the consensus had been that hospitals should operate at or below 85% capacity, so that there would be a margin to deal with unexpected pressures. Since the advent of Tory government in 2010, however, it seemed that austerity-driven politics had obliged hospitals to operate closer to 95% capacity. Throughput and maximum resource utilisation were apparently given priority over emergency readiness. Because of this, when the pandemic struck, the NHS had to function from a low base. Considerations of public health had taken second place to the need to keep taxes down and allow people the personal liberty to spend their money as they saw fit.

What was now evident was that the unpreparedness of an under-funded NHS would impact personal liberty to a much greater extent than modest tax increases would have done in the past. The cost of running the NHS with insufficient capacity was turning out to be very high indeed.

Newspapers were performing a useful function in highlighting these sorts of problems but the government should also have been being held to account by the official opposition. The Labour party's health spokesperson, Jonathan Ashworth, had been doing a pretty good job, but the party had yet to decide on its new leader and the gap at the top was making life too comfortable for the government.

The prolonged process for electing the new Labour Party leader finally came to an end on 4 April with the election by a huge majority of Sir Kier Starmer. It was a difficult time to take on the job of leader; at times of national crisis, parties are expected to work together for the common good. Accordingly, Sir Kier made it clear that he would not be opposing for the sake of opposing. However, he would be providing constructive opposition as this would be the best way to make sure the government was getting things right.

Among the issues to be flagged up early on was the delay in moving to social distancing. It had been clear from early statements by the government's Chief Scientific Adviser that the original approach had been to go for herd immunity. It was in that context that the Cheltenham Festival had been allowed to proceed from 16 to 19 March. With the huge numbers attending this event from Great Britain and Ireland and the attendant scope for spread of the virus, there could be no other explanation for the decision to proceed. And yet, four days later, the lockdown was announced. The government then denied that this represented a U-turn and insisted that there was never a policy of seeking herd immunity.

The UK government's hesitant approach to social distancing played into politics in Northern Ireland. The Irish government took a decision early on to follow WHO guidelines closely, moving to optimum levels of testing and closure of schools at an early stage. The UK appeared to cut back on testing once they had moved to the lockdown and they held back on closure of schools. Cracks then began to appear in Northern Ireland's governing Executive, with Sinn Fein arguing for an all-Ireland approach and adherence to WHO guidelines while the DUP was insistent that Northern Ireland should remain aligned with the advice coming from UK experts.

Closure of schools in Northern Ireland and the rest of the UK did take place a few days later but people were left wondering what the impact of the delay might have been on the spread of the virus.

The cracks in the Executive were papered over to some extent when a Memorandum of Understanding was signed, promising maximum coordination of Covid-19 strategies, north and south.

Things were no better at the UK level. At its daily press briefings, the government in London was coming under sustained pressure on two issues in particular – the low level of testing compared to other countries and the supply of PPE to front line staff. Ministers insisted that they were working hard and successfully on both issues but sceptical media representatives had little difficulty in demonstrating failure to meet testing targets and dissatisfaction of front-line staff working with inadequate PPE.

Like the rest of the population, Jim Kearney and his research colleagues from Scotland and the Republic of Ireland were following these developments with considerable interest. The existential threat posed to mankind by the pandemic was, of course, uppermost in their minds, as it was for everybody but, from their perspective, there was a subsidiary consideration. How would the twists and turns of the emergency and the relative performance of the different governments in tackling it affect attitudes to the constitutional project to be launched by the Gaelic Alliance?

This question was all the more relevant given what appeared to be Brexit related negative impacts on the British government's ability to control the virus. Arguably, there was never a worse time for a country to cut itself adrift from a successful international alliance than the eve of a pandemic requiring maximum global cooperation. One of the negative consequences of Brexit advanced by the Remain side (and discounted by the Leave side) had been the threat posed to availability of vital medicines originating in the EU or where key processes for making medicines available in the UK were controlled by the EU.

It is probable that few on the Remain side really expected these negative consequences to manifest themselves so early – even before the completion of the transition phase, and yet there now seemed to be little doubt that on several fronts (supply of ventilators, availability of PPE and availability of testing kits) the UK's semi-detached status relative to the EU had played a part in compromising the country's ability to function at optimal level. Given the global nature of the emergency, there was a strong international demand for key supplies and a limited supply. Those with the greatest purchasing power, such as the EU, would be in a position to outbid those with less purchasing power, like the UK.

Furthermore, it was reported in the media that Boris Johnson could have claimed from a £727 million pot to spend on supporting the NHS throughout the pandemic. The EU fund, originally established to offer support after natural disasters, such as earthquakes or flooding, was extended to cover the health emergency. The scheme was proposed to help member states to pay for much-needed personal protective equipment, development of vaccines and medicines and even public health checks. Seemingly, the UK could not bring itself to lodge an application for cash from the fund, despite the health benefits that would have accrued and despite having paid significant sums into it.

The UK would also have to shoulder the economic impact of the virus pandemic on its own, whereas Ireland and the other 26 remaining member states of the European

Union would be able to take advantage of a solidarity fund, to mitigate the effects of Covid-19. The fund, with initial funding of €500bn was announced in April 2020 (later increased to €750bn, comprising €390 in grants and €360 in loans).

Also, in April, Michel Barnier criticised the British government for its failure to properly address key issues related to the future of EU-UK trading relationships. The British refusal to contemplate any extension of the transition period beyond the end of 2020 (something that would need to be agreed before the end of June), whilst at the same time refusing to conduct the trade negotiations with any sense of urgency, was now in real danger of delivering a no-deal Brexit.

Depending on how all these Brexit-related negative developments played out over the remaining months of the emergency, there was no telling what impact they might have on the voting intentions of those participating in the planned Irish and Scottish referenda.

Another significant virus-related development during April occurred in the United States where Donald Trump was finding his normal style of bluster and denial politics was not working. During one of his daily press conferences, he suggested to the White House medical expert who was present that he had heard bleach-based disinfectants were effective in killing the virus and that the idea of injecting such products into infected individuals might be worth investigating. The expert was clearly appalled but said nothing. The media coverage in the succeeding days was excruciating for the president. He tried to suggest that he had been being sarcastic and had been quoted out of context by the fake-news media. Needless to say, this didn't wash as everybody watching the coverage of the press conference could see and hear exactly what had happened. The level of ridicule he was subjected to was bound to have an influence on his re-election chances later in the year.

The following month, media coverage of another Covid-19 related event, this time in the UK, resulted in humiliation for Dominic Cummings, Boris Johnson's chief advisor. It emerged that Cummings, who was 'very ill with symptoms of Covid-19' and who was supposed to be self-isolating, had made a 264-mile trip to Durham with his wife and young child. The trip was to his father's farm where he hoped to access childcare from his sister, in the event that he and his wife became incapacitated. Apparently, it was impossible to source childcare in London and so he had no alternative but to break the rules he had helped to make. Then when he was starting to recover and needed to get back to work, he drove 30 miles to the beauty spot of Barnard Castle with his wife and child to check whether his eyesight was good enough for the drive back to London! The date of this trip happened to coincide with his wife's birthday. At considerable cost, in terms of using up political capital, Boris Johnson refused to sack Cummings and indeed praised him, saying he had acted reasonably, legally and ethically. The long-suffering public who had made unimaginable sacrifices to keep to the rules, took note.

In May, the United Kingdom began to release lockdown restrictions, the degree of easing varying between countries. England was the most bullish going so far as to encourage a return to work where this could be done safely. Belatedly, there were increasing efforts to improve the test, trace and isolate strategy to pave the way for further easing of restrictions, in particular the reopening of schools. A parliamentary investigation began into the circumstances surrounding the government's decision to abandon test and trace at the time of the introduction of the lockdown. It had been noted that countries that had kept their test and trace strategies running alongside lockdown had outperformed the UK in keeping down rates of infection and deaths. In the UK, deaths of those testing positive for Covid-19 were now in excess of 40,000.

The UK now had the third highest rate of Covid-19 related infections in the world, with the United States occupying first position and Brazil, presided over by the Trump-like Jair Bolsonaro, in second position. Keir Starmer was putting Boris Johnson under increasing pressure in parliament as he moved from a generally supportive stance to one that probed the many delays and shortcomings presided over by the government. Johnson had had little difficulty in dealing with Jeremy Corbyn at Prime Minister's Questions but Starmer's forensic approach, honed during his time as Director of Public Prosecutions, left Johnson struggling on many occasions.

In June, Professor Neil Ferguson, argued that half of the 40,000 UK deaths from Covid-19 could have been avoided if the lockdown had been introduced a week earlier.

Around this time, the media began to focus on the relative performance of the UK government and the governments of the devolved administrations in the handling of the pandemic. Infection rates and death rates per 100,000 of the population were significantly lower in Northern Ireland, Scotland and Wales than in England, and the conclusion was being drawn that the decisions taken by the devolved administrations and the timing of those decisions had been instrumental in delivering better results. Vox pops conducted in the streets of Scotland and Northern Ireland suggested that the umbilical cord of unionism was being weakened by these revelations.

In mid-July, Boris Johnson responded to the many calls for a public enquiry into the government's handling of the Covid-19 pandemic and announced in Parliament that an enquiry would indeed be held – but not just yet! According to his logic, now was not the time to divert attention from tacking the emergency. In the view of most people, now was precisely the time for the enquiry, as any lessons learned could be taken account of in handling future waves of the infection! The disadvantage for the government would, of course, be that ministers would still be in office when being held to account for their performance.

An enquiry would undoubtedly have to take place at some stage and among the issues to be addressed would certainly be the government's handling of contact tracing – a critical function for facilitating the easing of lockdown. In England, this had been largely ineffective, with shortcomings including the failure of a bespoke NHS contact-tracing app for mobile phones. By contrast, a successful contact-tracing app went live in Northern Ireland at the end of July. This app was compatible with an app in the Republic of Ireland and was the first example in the world of a contact-tracing app that could operate across an international border.

*****

The first sign that the comfortable 80-seat Tory majority in parliament might not forever ensure a comfortable life for the Prime Minister came when he was forced to do a U-turn on policy related to NHS provision for immigrants from outside the EU. The plan had been to charge such immigrants, including those who had been working heroically for the NHS during the pandemic, an annual fee of £400 per person for access to services. This crass policy was opposed strongly by the Labour Party and by sufficient rebellious Tories to force a change of heart. Jim Kearney and his Delphi colleagues took note of this promising straw in the wind!

The Government's understandable preoccupation with the Covid-19 crisis had resulted in minimal progress with UK-EU trade talks. Pressure on Johnson to seek an extension of the transition period beyond the end of 2020 intensified as 30 June, the last date for requesting an extension, approached. It was clear to all objective commentators that the chances of concluding a satisfactory trade deal without an extension were remote. The clamour was to no avail, however, and June came and went without any request being made. A no-deal Brexit now seemed unavoidable.

In July, the prospects for international trade took another hit when the UK was forced to renege on the agreement to involve the Chinese firm Huawei in the roll out of 5G communications technology. Huawei was already involved in 3G and 4G and a significant investment had been made in the incorporation of Huawei equipment in the infrastructure for 5G. The Trump administration in the US was involved in an escalating trade war with China and it had been putting pressure on the UK to follow its lead in boycotting Huawei 'on grounds of national security'.

Finally, the UK had succumbed to this pressure and moved to ban any new investment by Huawei from the end of 2020. Existing Huawei equipment would be removed by the end of 2027 at enormous cost – not only financially but also in terms of slowing down the implementation of 5G technology throughout the UK. China's response indicated that there would be a big price to pay for this decision down the line, including prospects for a beneficial UK-China trade deal, which were now dead in the water.

This episode was a clear demonstration of the vacuity of the Brexiteer dream of 'taking back control'. What had happened, in fact, was that the UK had given up its shared control of European affairs and exchanged it for UK subservience to the USA.

The trade talks with the EU staggered on throughout July before being dealt a blow in late August when Boris Johnson decided to renege on the commitments contained in the Withdrawal Agreement designed to avoid a hard border on the island of Ireland. In the run up to the December 2019 general election, this agreement had been described by Johnson as an excellent oven-ready deal and one which would 'get Brexit done'. It was clear to everyone that the deal would require some controls on trade between Great Britain and Northern Ireland but this was denied by Johnson. Now he argued that this aspect of the agreement was due to intransigence by the EU and was completely unacceptable. Accordingly, his government introduced a UK internal market bill which would seek to prevent any sort of border in the Irish Sea in contravention of the international agreement they had signed with the EU. The bill faced strong opposition from the Labour Party, government back-benchers and five ex-Prime Ministers who argued that the measure was an embarrassment which would destroy the UK's international reputation and make it difficult to conclude the trade deals so vital to the UK, post-Brexit. Nevertheless, the bill passed into law in September, thanks in part to support from the DUP. The debacle also poisoned the atmosphere of the UK/EU trade talks. In the United States, Senate Speaker, Nancy Pelosi, issued a warning that Congress would block any trade deal between the UK and the USA, if an open border on the island of Ireland was threatened by Boris Johnson's reckless shredding of the Withdrawal Agreement. Several Democrat congressmen wrote to Boris Johnson in similar terms and Joe Biden, the Democratic candidate for President issued the same warning. On 1 October, the EU started legal action against the UK for breaking the international Withdrawal Agreement.

By this time, a second wave of the Covid-19 pandemic was gathering pace and increasing numbers of infections and hospitalisations were occurring in the UK and Ireland and in a number of other countries in Europe and further afield. Having performed relatively well in the first wave of the pandemic, Northern Ireland was now in the invidious position of having the highest infection rate in the British Isles. The Irish counties bordering Northern Ireland – Donegal, Cavan and Monaghan – had the highest rates in the Republic, suggesting that cross-border movements were contributing to spread of the infection.

It seemed self-evident that alignment of measures to control the virus on both sides of the Irish border would improve the chances of success. There had always been a common animal health regime on the island of Ireland and this had helped to ensure that epidemics of animal diseases, such as foot and mouth and fowl pest were kept to a minimum. This was proving difficult to achieve in the case of Covid-19, due mainly to Northern Ireland's position as part of the United Kingdom. The Republic was in a position to move quickly to impose restrictions recommended by its medical and scientific advisors and to deal with the economic consequences of those restrictions. Northern Ireland was in a more difficult position because it could not automatically access the funding necessary to facilitate parallel measures.

In this second wave, the Republic decided to close all non-essential retail outlets and to compensate the shop owners for the economic hit. Because shops were not being closed in England, the Treasury was not ready to give Northern Ireland the funding needed to close shops in Northern Ireland. Shops north of the border therefore remained open, providing an obvious temptation for people in the Republic to cross the border and continue shopping – even if that was difficult because of a five-kilometre limit in the Republic on the distance people could travel from their homes.

Here was yet another negative experience that conceivably could impact on the voting intentions of those participating in the planned Irish border poll.

The future voting intentions of 'red wall' conservatives in northern constituencies were also likely to be impacted by the latest Covid-19 developments in England. When the virulent second wave of the pandemic struck, the government introduced a new three-tier system under which regions of England would be designated as 'medium', 'high' or 'very high', depending on the rate of infection. The 'very high' category involved severe restrictions leading to significant loss of employment. Liverpool was the first city to be included in this category, followed by Manchester and wider Lancashire. There were objections from Labour leaders in these locations on the grounds that they had not been properly consulted and that inadequate financial compensation was in place for those who would lose their jobs. They made the point that this would represent 'levelling down' rather than the promised 'levelling up', which had featured so prominently in Boris Johnson's pitch to red wall voters in the 2019 general election.

*****

In the United States, the elaborate electoral process for the election of the 46th president was moving towards a climax and things were not looking good for Donald J. Trump. He had behaved badly in relation to protests in June against racist police brutality that had resulted in the death of George Floyd in Minneapolis. Instead of displaying empathy or attempting to bring people together, he defined the protests as domestic terrorism and threatened to bring in the army to quell the disturbances. Peaceful protesters in front of the White House were cleared using tear gas so that Trump could reach a church across the road for a photo opportunity – looking tough and holding a bible aloft!

Other affronts included cutting off funding to the US Postal Service in an attempt to thwart postal voting in the upcoming election (postal voting being seen as favouring the Democrats), and a gratuitous insult to veterans of the First World War whom he was reported to have described as 'losers'.

Poll results began to move in favour of the Democrats, suggesting that this behaviour and his performance during the pandemic had been too much even for his erstwhile loyal supporters in the rust belt. Then, in early October, the chickens came home to roost when Trump and First Lady Melania Trump tested positive for Covid-19. They had been involved in a recent event at the White House celebrating the nomination of a right-wing justice to replace the liberal Ruth Bader Ginsburg who had died on 19 September. Justice Ginsburg's dying wish had been that action to replace her would be delayed until after the presidential election. Her wishes were ignored and the Republicans proceeded with the nomination. At the White House celebrations, there was no social distancing and no facemasks were worn. The end result was that more than 20 people became infected, including the president and first lady.

Trump was given a range of medications, including an experimental drug that had yet to be approved for public use. He made a miraculous recovery, prompting some to wonder if he had really been infected in the first place! His first action on recovery was to head for Florida, an important swing-state for the forthcoming election, where he held a mass rally, without social distancing and without face masks. He declared himself immune, powerful and ready to come into the crowd and give everybody 'a big fat kiss'! All of which played well with his core supporters but alienated the floating voters he needed to attract.

The date of the Presidential election was 3 November but voting by post (mail-in ballots) was permitted in advance of this date. Attitudes to the Covid-19 virus played a part in how the election would unfold. Democrats were more risk-averse and opted in significant numbers for postal voting. Republicans were influenced by Trump's gung-ho attitude and preferred the option of voting in person on the day.

When the votes cast on 3 November were tallied up, it appeared that Trump was on course to be re-elected. In fact, he declared as much on 4 November. As expected, however, when the mail-in ballots started to be counted, the position began to change. These ballots were overwhelmingly Democrat and slowly but surely Joe Biden began to make ground, eventually overtaking Trump in key battleground states in the south and in the rust-belt. On 7 November, Biden passed the key figure of 270 electoral college votes and was elected the 46th US President. Biden had succeeded in taking back the traditionally Democrat states in the rust-belt that had been won by Trump in 2016, and winning a number of states in the south which had been traditional Republican states for many years.

Trump turned out to be a bad loser and launched a series of legal challenges, claiming irregularities and fraudulent voting linked to the mail-in ballots. He offered no evidence of this and continued to cry foul during much of the hand-over period when he should have been facilitating the transfer of power to the new administration. Towards the end of November, under the influence of grown-ups in the Republican Party, he conceded that hand-over arrangements could begin, facilitating the transfer of power to Joe Biden.

As a face-saving exercise, he would continue to pursue a number of doomed legal challenges.

There had been an earlier excruciating moment on 9 November when the pharmaceutical firm Pfizer, in partnership with BioNTech of Germany, announced positive results of the trials of their mRNA-based vaccine against Covid-19. The vaccine was proving 90% effective in protecting against Covid-19 infection and the whole world reacted joyfully to the news that might herald an end to the pandemic nightmare. Trump's reaction was to claim credit for the development which had taken place 'under his watch'. Pfizer quickly responded with a categorical denial that Trump or his government had had anything to do with development of the vaccine.

Back in the UK, another sign of the easing of political dysfunctionality appeared on 13 November when Dominic Cummings was unceremoniously ejected from Downing Street. He and his fellow Brexiteers, who had been advising Boris Johnson on government policy since the December 2019 Tory election victory, had apparently been caught out briefing the media against the Prime Minister. Cummings was filmed leaving Number 10 carrying the contents of his desk in a cardboard box. This was a bittersweet moment for the sensible middle ground in politics. On the one hand, it was great to witness the departure of this malign influence from the heart of government, on the other hand, he had already achieved his objective and there was little prospect of turning the clock back on the Brexit debacle.

Despite Cummings's departure, it was no surprise that the UK-EU trade talks became bogged down in December. The UK was still having difficulty grasping the reality that it was impossible to have full sovereignty and, at the same time, full access to the EU's internal market. The two sides became deadlocked on access for European fishing fleets to UK waters and the fact that, in return for a zero-tariff trade deal, Britain would be required to adhere to the EU's developing state aid rules and common environmental, social and labour standards. On 8 December, the UK came to its senses on the issue of the Northern Ireland protocol and dropped the legislation designed to override its provisions. Arrangements for managing trade between Great Britain and Northern Ireland post-Brexit were finally agreed. This had the effect of improving relations between the two sides, and after many twists and turns, a UK/EU trade deal of sorts – known as an association agreement – was arrived at on 24 December.

The agreement was far from the success trumpeted by Johnson, however, and could best be described as a damage limitation exercise. To the dismay of the UK fishing industry, Johnson's negotiators had had to agree to significant continuing access to British waters for EU fishing fleets. On trade, Britain would have the right to diverge from EU rules in the future (thereby 'taking back control'), but doing so would be likely to lead to loss of the benefits of the trade agreement, with tariffs being re-imposed (thereby losing control again!). The UK also failed to win the argument that would allow imported foreign parts, such as car components from Japan and other non-EU sources, to count towards the agreement's 'rules of origin' thresholds, which determine whether a product (such as a British-manufactured car) may or may not be traded tariff-free.

Other failures included absence of agreement on trading services (as opposed to goods) which account for 80% of the British economy and less-than-comprehensive arrangements for security cooperation, data sharing and mutual recognition of professional qualifications.

The Pangolin is the suspected intermediate host for the
transmission of the Covid-19 virus (Creative Commons Attribution
– Share Alike 2.0 Generic (CC-BY-SA-2.0))

Donald Trump's Covid-19 press briefings never failed to shock
and embarrass. The faces of his officials tell it all!
(Creative Commons Public Domain Mark 1.0)

Kier Starmer was elected Labour Party leader on 4 April 2020
(Creative Commons Attribution 2.0 Generic (CC-BY-2.0))

Joe Biden was elected 46th US President on7 November 2020
(Copyright Cage Skidmore; Creative Commons Attribution –
ShareAlike 2.0 Generic (CC-BY-SA-2.0))

Chapter 8
The Gaelic Alliance

The year 2021 began with more shocking developments in the world of Donald Trump. With only two weeks to go until his scheduled departure from the White House, on 6 January, he made an inflammatory speech again accusing the Democrats of stealing the election from him and appearing to encourage his supporters to march on the Capitol building in Washington where Congress was in the process of certifying Joe Bidon's victory. The mob duly complied and stormed the building, overpowering the police guard, running amok through the corridors and vandalising offices and the debating chambers. One policeman and four rioters died. Once the mob had dispersed, members of Congress resumed their work, continuing through the night to complete the certification process.

In the following days, erstwhile loyal Republican supporters finally started distancing themselves from Trump and moves began to initiate the process of impeaching the president for a second time, a process that would be made easier this time around thanks to recent run-off elections in Georgia, that were won by the Democrats, giving them control of the Senate. In the end, although he was impeached, sufficient Republicans in the Senate rallied to the cause to prevent the two-thirds majority needed for conviction.

*****

Boris Johnson's decision to take the UK out of the EU on 31 December with a minimalist trade agreement caused a significant shock and had the effect of re-dividing the country after the degree of coming together that had resulted from the Covid-19 pandemic.

Several opinion polls published in the first half of 2021 showed that just under half of the population approved of the slim-deal exit, with slightly more opposed. On the issue of Brexit itself, a majority now accepted the reality of the UK's independence while about one third would continue to support eventual re-entry to the EU. Scotland and Northern Ireland continued to buck the trend with significant majorities in both countries opposed to both the fact and the nature of the UK's departure.

Following the commencement of the Covid-19 vaccination programme in December 2020 and the on/off easing of restrictions, Jim Kearney and his colleagues were able to make some progress on the establishment of the Gaelic Alliance. It was agreed that the alliance should be organised in each of the three countries of the planned federation and that there should be a national secretary and a national president in each.

As he now had a secure academic position at Ulster University, Jim felt he was well placed to take on the role of Northern Ireland secretary, at least for an initial period. Niall Murphy and Angus Crawford were in a more difficult position because of their public sector positions. An obvious solution was arrived at - Mary Douglas and Sean Donnelly would take on the secretary role in Scotland and the Irish Republic.

More critical to the success of the initiative would be the identification of inspirational and charismatic individuals to fill the presidential role in each jurisdiction. Jim, Mary and Sean took on the task of finding suitable candidates. As the presidential role would be an essentially political one, the search would need to concentrate on identifying potential fellow travellers within existing political parties.

It was fairly clear that some parties would provide more promising recruiting ground than others. In the case of Northern Ireland, the Alliance Party seemed like the best place to start, and so Jim set about sounding out Alliance politicians he knew to be capable of thinking outside the box. What he was looking for was a rising star – someone with potential who had yet to make it to the top echelons of the party. After several non-productive meetings, Jim met with Jane Harrington, a prospective Alliance parliamentary candidate for one of the Belfast constituencies. It didn't take too much persuasion to convince Jane that this was an opportunity that could well fast-forward her political career. Before committing herself Jane wanted to run the idea past senior party members. Jim fully understood her caution and indeed welcomed the opportunity to get some feedback on the likely attitude of the Alliance party to the federation concept.

The feedback was very encouraging. Not only did the party support the idea of Jane taking on the role of Northern

Ireland president but they were quite enthusiastic about the whole concept of the Gaelic Federation!

Another surprising outcome of Jim's networking was that the reaction of the other Northern Ireland political parties was less dyed-in-the-wool than might have been expected. Unsurprisingly, the SDLP and the Greens were reasonably positive and the Ulster Unionists were undecided. It was the reaction of the DUP and Sinn Fein that caused the greatest shock. Most members of both parties showed vehement opposition to the whole concept – for diametrically opposed reasons – but a significant proportion showed some level of interest in the idea. For the DUP, the attraction was that there would be a continuing link with Scotland – the UK country with which Northern Ireland had the strongest affinity – while for Sinn Fein, the attraction was that the federation would involve separation from England.

Down south, Sean Donnelly found a similar mix of reactions but with a healthy level of overall support for the idea. Fine Gael members showed the strongest support and it was a prospective Fine Gael candidate for a Cork constituency, Maeve McDermott, who stepped up to the mark, agreeing to act as interim Gaelic Alliance president for the Republic.

Mary Douglas expected strong opposition from the Scottish Conservatives and Labour and she was not disappointed. The Liberal Democrats were also less than enthusiastic. There was a mixed reaction from the Scottish Nationalists, mirroring the Sinn Fein attitude in Ireland, but some could see that, for many Scots, this might be a more attractive route to independence than going it alone. John

Campbell, a Scottish National Party councillor from Ayrshire, checked out the likely attitude of the party before accepting the role of Alliance president for Scotland. An official position would eventually have to be taken but, at this stage, it seemed likely that the party would allow campaigning for Scottish independence with or without the Irish connection. In that event, individual SNP members would be able to make their own mind up which route to support.

Boris Johnston and his cabinet colleagues were still making bullish pronouncements about the prospects for the UK economy now that the country was free of the shackles of the EU. The reality looked a little different. With the Covid-19 pandemic continuing, albeit at a reducing level, the country was up to its ears in debt and absence of freedom of movement was resulting in severe staff shortages in many sectors. There was no money in the kitty from which to fund the levelling up promised to new Conservative constituencies in the north of England. On top of this, there were very few trade deals in place.

In April there was further bad news for the Conservatives when it emerged that funds for the refurbishment of Boris Johnson's apartment at No 11 Downing Street might have come from suspect sources, possibly a Tory donor. Three separate enquiries were set up in an attempt to get to the bottom of the matter. In another damning development it was revealed by several unnamed sources that Johnson had made the comment that he would "rather see bodies piling high in the streets" than agree to another Covid lockdown.

On 6 May, a series of elections took place throughout Great Britain including parliamentary elections in England and Wales, a by-election in the Labour-held seat of Hartlepool, numerous council elections in England, mayoral elections in London and a number of other metropolitan areas and police and crime commissioner elections in England and Wales. In Scotland the SNP gained ground but fell one seat short of an overall majority. The pro-independence Green Party won eight seats so there would still be a majority for a new independence referendum. In Wales, the Labour Party won 30 out of 60 seats and would continue in government.

Given the unrelenting bad news the UK government had been experiencing, the English results came as something of a shock for the Labour Party. Although Labour did well in the mayoral elections, the Tories took Hartlepool, a seat that had been held by Labour since its inception, and there was also a big swing towards the Conservatives in many council areas, especially in the north of England. There seemed to be two explanations for these astonishing results.

Firstly despite, in the view of many, having made a mess of virtually every aspect of the fight against Covid-19 resulting in one of the highest death rates in the world, the Government was now being given credit for an excellent vaccination programme. Although the real credit was due to the scientists who had created the vaccines and the NHS who had managed the vaccination roll out very effectively, Johnson's government gained sufficient reflected glory to obliterate their past litany of mistakes in the minds of the voters.

Secondly, it was evident from an analysis of the results that most of the Tory gains had come from voters who had previously voted for the Brexit Party. Brexit Party votes had transferred to the closest available alternative – the Conservative Party.

It was clear from these results that English nationalists were as enamoured as ever with the Brexit project. The mayhem that the fallout from Brexit had caused to politics in Northern Ireland, with the DUP tearing itself apart over the issue of the Northern Ireland Protocol and how best to oppose it, was far from their thoughts. Arlene Foster's misplaced trust in Johnson's pledge not to countenance a border in the Irish Sea had now cost her her job as DUP Leader and First Minister. Her replacement as party leader, Edwin Poots, was elected on a promise to dismantle the Northern Ireland Protocol! Four weeks later Poots was in turn deposed as a result of what his party saw as unwarranted concessions to Sinn Féin. He was replaced by Jeffrey Donaldson. The fragile peace process was experiencing significant destabilisation.

It seemed to Jim Kearney and his colleagues that there would never be a more propitious time to launch the campaign for Irish unification, Scottish independence and consolidation of links with the European Union.

Now that the key positions in the Gaelic Alliance had been filled, a strategy would have to be developed for taking the initiative forward. To get the ball rolling, the six post-holders agreed to meet up in Belfast for a three-day brainstorming session at the beginning of July. The venue was a conference room at the Belfast city centre campus of Ulster University. They agreed to rotate the chairmanship,

111

with Jane Harrington kicking off on the morning of day one. An agenda had been prepared by Jim:

1. Financing of the Alliance
2. Building membership
3. Launch event
4. Other awareness-raising events
5. Date for AGM
6. Timetable for the referenda
7. Information document for the referenda
8. Strategy for influencing governments
9. AOB

There would be two main routes to building up the funds that would be needed to finance the organisation and its campaigns: sponsorship by supportive individuals and companies and membership fees. Each of the presidents was given the task of identifying interested donors in their respective territories. On the question of membership, there was a lengthy discussion as to whether the membership fee should be kept low, to attract the maximum number of members, or high to ensure a committed membership. In the end, the decision was to pitch the fee around the same level as the mainstream political parties – £50 / €60 a year.

On membership numbers, it was felt that there would be little movement until after the official launch of the organisation but, given a fair wind and an inspirational campaign, a figure of 250,000 members by the middle of 2022 seemed a reasonable target to aim for.

The launch event would be critical to the success of the initiative. To ensure sufficient media interest, it would be important to avoid clashing with other significant political events. One way to achieve this would be to select a date during the autumn parliamentary recess when there were unlikely to be many competing political stories. A decision was taken to launch the Alliance on Thursday 28 October 2021. Jim Kearney was given the job of putting together a press release to be issued in the run up to the launch event. The draft would be shared with other members of the group before finalisation.

John Campbell took over the chairmanship on day two and the group moved to discussion of other awareness raising events. The various pro-EU marches organised during 2019 had been very successful in raising the profile of the People's Vote campaign even if, in the end, they had not led to a successful outcome for Remainers, and so it was agreed that several high-profile marches in Scotland and in Ireland (north and south) could be an effective way of making the public aware of the Gaelic Alliance and its objectives. It would be important to get the timing right, as premature events engendering limited media interest could be counter-productive. Mid-December would allow six weeks after the launch for interest to build up and sufficient time for the Covid-19 vaccination programme to be completed, making mass gatherings safe again. During this period, the three presidents would do as much political networking and do as many media interviews as possible. An opinion poll would be organised at the end of November and would hopefully play a part in building up expectations for a successful series of marches.

The main item on the agenda for the AGM would be the election of office bearers, recognising that the inaugural post-holders had not been identified democratically. The group felt, however, that it could be disruptive to make changes to the team too early on and that momentum could be lost during those critical early months if the AGM was held prematurely. Late-January was eventually selected, as this would allow a few weeks of activity guided by the enthusiastic start-up group before any potential personnel changes. The hope would be of course that the membership would endorse the existing team and give them a mandate to continue leading the campaign throughout 2022.

The other main item on the agenda of the AGM would be the programme of activities for 2022, including a target date for the referenda, for which the Alliance would be pressing.

In terms of timing, the aim would be to hold the referenda before the end of 2022, or early 2023. Much would depend on the attitude of the British government in particular. They could be expected to be strongly resistant, as had already been signalled by their refusal to agree to a second Scottish independence referendum. A strategy for persuading the British government to move on the issue would need to be developed and might include finding pressure points where international influence could be brought to bear.

On day three, Maeve McDermott took over the chair with only one remaining item on the agenda – the issue of developing an information document that would ensure the public would be voting from a position of knowledge rather than one of ignorance combined with sound bites and slogans. The first Scottish independence referendum would be used as a guide and every effort would be made to produce a document comparable to the one used for that vote. This would be in contrast to the Brexit referendum, where no such document had been produced and where the information vacuum had been filled by misinformation, sound bites, foreign interference and internet manipulation. Not only did the voters not have an objective guide as to what Brexit might really look like but the Leave campaign itself was found to be in the dark on the way ahead when they were faced with an unexpected victory.

All the key concerns likely to be on the minds of voters would have to be fully discussed and analysed in the information document. These would include the economic prospects for the new federation, its social framework, including organisation and funding of health and social services, security of pensions, currency considerations, EU accession issues and relationships between the federal parliament and the Scottish and Irish national parliaments. A framework document, addressing these and many other issues would need to be prepared by the three secretaries and cleared with the three presidents for tabling at the AGM in January. Work would then need to continue to put meat on the bones and ensure that a comprehensive document would be ready in good time for the referenda – hopefully in late 2022.

Under Any Other Business, Jim raised the issue of a logo for the Gaelic Alliance and proposed that a combination of the crosses of St Patrick and St Andrew might be a neat way of encapsulating the scope of the initiative. This would effectively be the union jack with the cross of St George removed. As well as being an appropriate logo for the Alliance, this flag might eventually be accepted as the flag of the Gaelic Federation. All were in agreement with Jim's proposal.

In the third week of July, following the conclusion of what all agreed was a successful brainstorming meeting, Jim began work on the press release which was to be issued to the media at the end of the month. A draft was circulated to other members of the core group and an agreed version was issued on 20 August:

Launch of the Gaelic Alliance

An initiative will be launched on 28 October aimed at restoring EU membership to the disenfranchised populations of Scotland and Northern Ireland.

The Gaelic Alliance will campaign for coterminous referenda to be held in Scotland and Ireland (north and south), giving voters in each country three choices for their constitutional future. In Scotland, the choice will be between the status quo, Scottish independence or Scottish independence within the context of a federation with Ireland. In Ireland, the choice will be between the status quo, a united Ireland or a united Ireland within the context of a federation with Scotland.

The Alliance will campaign in the first instance for agreement to hold the referenda and, once agreement has been secured, will campaign for the option of a Gaelic Federation of Ireland and Scotland.

The official launch of the Gaelic Alliance will take place on 28 October 2021 and the target date for the referenda will be the end of 2022.

Membership of the Alliance is already open and those interested can join for an annual membership fee of £50 or €60 (www.gaelicalliance.com/membership).

Interim national presidents of the Alliance:

John Campbell – Scotland

Jane Harrington – Northern Ireland

Maeve McDermott – Republic of Ireland

will be available for media interviews between now and the official launch to explain more about the initiative and its objectives.

Further information can be obtained from the interim national secretaries:

Mary Douglas – Scotland

(mary_douglas@hotmail.com)

Sean Donnelly – Republic of Ireland

(seandonnelly@aol.com)

Jim Kearney – Northern Ireland

(jkearney@gmail.com)

The press release got a huge amount of coverage both in the papers and on the broadcast media and created a storm of interest in all countries of the British Isles. The three national presidents were in great demand and appeared on all the main news channels in Britain and Ireland. A theme running through all the interviews was that the concept of a Gaelic Federation could represent a win-win situation for all the countries of the United Kingdom, with the possible exception of Wales.

Opinion polls in England had shown on several occasions that the majority of the population would shed very few tears if Scotland and Northern Ireland were to leave the Union and achievement of Brexit was certainly much higher up the list of English priorities than keeping the Union together. In Scotland and Ireland, north and south, there was a strong affinity with the European Union and the proposed Gaelic Federation would ensure that EU membership would be extended from the Republic of Ireland to the populations of the other two Alliance jurisdictions. Wales was in a slightly invidious position, having voted in favour of Brexit and then come to regret it.

On the back of the extensive media coverage, membership applications began to flood in, as did offers of financial support from Europhile companies and organisations. By the time of the launch event on 28 October, the membership stood at 15,790 and the Alliance had £1.47m in the bank.

The launch took place at the Waterfront Hall in Belfast and again media interest was intense, not only from the UK and Ireland but from many countries around the world, including the United States, most countries in Europe and several countries in Asia, notably China and Japan. Positive coverage of the event was beamed around the world in the following days.

The concept of a win-win situation had not found its way through to the British government. Boris Johnson and a number of senior cabinet members did a round of interviews following the launch and gave the thumbs down to the whole idea. There was no way they were going to agree to an Irish border poll or another Scottish Independence referendum, with or without the inclusion of a federation option.

Jim and his colleagues weren't too concerned by this for the moment. There was a long way to go and the Johnson administration was coming under ever-increasing pressure resulting from the dire economic legacy of Covid-19 and emerging negative consequences of Brexit. A shortage of lorry drivers in the autumn led to problems with the supply chain for many products. Fuel supplies were badly affected with many petrol stations running out of petrol and diesel. The ending of freedom of movement was clearly a contributory factor and the Government was forced to introduce an emergency visa programme to encourage lorry drivers from the EU to come back to the UK. The measure was largely ineffective. Shortages of many products in the run-up to Christmas were predicted.

Northern Ireland had already been experiencing shortages of some products due to the impact of the Northern Ireland Protocol. The EU expressed its willingness to explore technical adjustments to ease these problems but the Brexit minister, Lord Frost (ennobled for his part in taking the UK out of the European Union) preferred loudspeaker diplomacy, threatening to torpedo the Protocol by invoking Article 16 of the Withdrawal Agreement.

Tory MPs from the north of England were also becoming increasingly frustrated by the government's failure to deliver on the promised levelling up for their constituencies. Divisions were occurring within the ranks of the governing party from time to time, including a major fracture in relation to censure of Tory MP Owen Patterson who had been found guilty by the Commons Standards Committee of breaking lobbying rules. The Government tried to overturn the proposed censure, arguing that the process was unfair and needed to be reformed. The move provoked outrage in parliament, including from many in the Conservative Party. The possibility of further defeats on particular issues could not be ruled out. and there was every chance that, in due course, the Alliance and its supporters in Westminster would be able to apply pressure to the government to adopt a more reasonable attitude to the political developments in Scotland and Ireland.

International pressure might also be brought to bear. President Biden's administration was particularly supportive of the federation initiative and promised to provide whatever support they could to give it a fair wind. The UK was working on a comprehensive trade deal with the US and it was conceivable that continuing UK government intransigence in relation to the border and independence polls could lead to Irish American pressure in the US to withhold agreement to the conclusion of the deal.

The British government was already encountering difficulties with other trade deal negotiations and was finding that the mantra 'take back control' was difficult to deliver in practice. In the case of India, a deal was well advanced but was being held up because of British reluctance to accede to Indian demands for a relaxation of the conditions for granting of student visas. A deal with

China was also held back because of UK government criticism of China's treatment of the Uyghur Muslims in the Xinjiang autonomous region and because of a demand that Huawei be allowed to resume its role in the development of 5G telecommunications in the UK, against the wishes of many MPs in both the governing and opposition parties.

All of this was grist to the mill of those pursuing the Gaelic Federation initiative. It used to be said that 'England's difficulty is Ireland's opportunity'. This could now be re-envisioned to read 'England's difficulty is the Gaelic Federation's opportunity'.

With six weeks to go before the first series of awareness-raising marches was scheduled to take place, the GA committee members turned their attention to planning and organising those events and the opinion poll that was to pre-date them. Marches were to be held in Edinburgh, Belfast and Dublin and individual planning groups would be needed for each. Members were circulated, asking for volunteers and no difficulties were experienced in putting together three enthusiastic groups, chaired by Mary Crawford, Jim Kearney and Sean Donnelly. The polling organisation Opinium was approached and agreed to arrange a pre-march opinion poll at the end of November, using the question sets from the Round 4 Delphi Survey. If the results were anything like those from the Delphi survey, this would be a great scene-setter for a successful series of marches.

The Alliance was still engendering plenty of positive publicity with John Campbell, Jane Harrington and Maeve McDermott in constant demand from all corners of the media. It was looking less and less likely that Boris

Johnson's government would be able to sustain their anti-referendum stance for much longer.

By the middle of November, the work of the three groups planning the marches was well advanced and publicity material was being developed, announcing the timing and routes for the marches and arrangements for assembling on the chosen day – Wednesday 15 December. The Scottish supporters would assemble in Princes Street in the centre of Edinburgh and march to the Scottish Parliament Building at Holyrood; the Northern Ireland supporters would assemble at the City Hall in the centre of Belfast and march to Parliament Buildings, Stormont; and the Irish supporters would assemble at Ballsbridge, on the south side of Dublin, and march to Leinster House.

The media reaction to the planned marches unfolded along predictable lines, very much as it had done during the Brexit and post-Brexit periods. The right-wing press was generally hostile while the Mirror, Guardian, Observer and especially The New European were very supportive.

The results of the Opinium poll were published on 2 December and, as expected, provided a perfect backdrop for the impending marches.

	NI	RoI	Scotland
Status quo:	31%	19%	29%
United Ireland:	23%	39%	
Independent Scotland:			33%
Gaelic Federation:	46%	42%	38%

The 15th of December dawned cool but sunny, and big crowds were soon assembling at the starting points in

Edinburgh, Belfast and Dublin. Television crews from many countries were present at each location and pictures of the massing crowds were being beamed around the world. Many high-profile celebrities attended the rallies at all three locations and made stirring speeches from the podiums, as did the three GA presidents.

Coverage of the marches on television and in the press was extensive, with attitudes dividing on predictable lines. The right-wing tabloids played down the numbers while the left-wing press and the main TV channels were more upbeat and generally supportive. Senior cabinet members were again mobilised to deliver the customary dose of cold water. Objective observers estimated the number of marchers at around 900,000 spread over the three sites.

In the months following the marches, the concept of the Gaelic Federation continued to gain traction and the UK Government continued its policy of strong resistance. Their focus was, in any case, on other things, notably on efforts to conclude trade deals with the United States and other significant economic players in an attempt to mitigate the effects of disrupted access to the European single market. The negotiations were proving difficult, as potential trading partners were demanding concessions the UK was not ready to give.

Things were progressing better with the United States and, by October, a draft deal had been put together by the two negotiating teams, ready to be signed off at political level. Unfortunately, for Boris Johnson, President Biden had been coming under mounting pressure from the Irish American lobby in connection with the developments in the UK and Ireland surrounding the proposed Gaelic Federation.

This pressure manifested itself in the introduction of a US caveat, tabled at the first head-to-head meeting between Biden and Johnson. In essence, the caveat stated that the deal would not be concluded unless the UK government agreed to the running of an Irish border poll and a referendum on Scottish Independence.

Johnson had no option but to capitulate, and on 16 November, the government tabled a motion in Parliament paving the way for the running of the two polls by the end of 2022. The motion was approved by a substantial majority in both Houses.

The Scottish Parliament Building, Holyrood
(Creative Commons Attribution – ShareAlike 2.0 Generic (CC-BY-SA-2.0))

Parliament Buildings, Stormont
(creative Commons Attribution – ShareAlike 2.0 Generic (CC-BY-SA-2.0))

Leinster House, Dublin

Chapter 9
Referendum Year, 2022

Jim Kearney and the other members of the Gaelic Alliance Executive Committee were jubilant and, following a few days of justifiable celebration, turned their attention to the planning of the Annual General Meeting, due to be held on 27 January. They couldn't have hoped for a better context in which to progress the business of the AGM. It was held at the Waterfront Hall, Belfast and attracted big numbers from all three jurisdictions. The 1½-day meeting was chaired by the three GA Presidents in rotation, with Jane Harrington kicking off on the morning of day 1.

Election of office bearers was the first item on the agenda and to the great relief of Jim Kearney and his colleagues the reaction of the delegates to the work of the interim office bearers was universally positive. All were agreed that things couldn't have gone better over the first two months of the Alliance's existence. The recent capitulation of the British government over the Scottish and Irish polls represented a major feather in the cap of the interim committee. The voting went smoothly and all six interim office bearers were elected unopposed to serve for the year 2022.

John Campbell took over the chair for the afternoon session and the meeting moved to consider the programme of activities for 2022. It was clear to all concerned that the programme would need to be geared to building momentum throughout the year towards the holding of the Irish border poll and the Scottish independence referendum.

The profile of the organisation would also need to be maintained and it was agreed that a further series of marches should be organised throughout the year alongside as many media interviews as possible by members of the Executive Committee.

If the referenda were to be held by December 2022 there would be a lot of work to be done to reassure the public about the range of concerns that had been flagged up during the Delphi surveys of 2019/20. These included worries about economic performance, currencies, health and social care provision, pensions, cross-border trade and inter-community conflict. An information document would need to be prepared for distribution to the populations of Scotland and Ireland (north and south) in advance of the polls. This would ensure that people would be voting with full knowledge of all relevant facts.

There was a lively debate about all of these issues for the remainder of day 1, extending into the morning of day 2 when Maeve McDermott took over the chair. The meeting concluded that concerns about the economy could best be addressed by including some comparisons of economic performance in the different jurisdictions, noting that Ireland was currently out-performing the UK on growth rate and a number of other key indicators. Currency concerns could also be dealt with by referencing Ireland's bounce back from the 2008 recession and its impressive post-Covid performance – both of which had been assisted by its membership of the single currency.

On health and social care, the delegates mandated the GA secretariat to carry out some research into models of health care in Europe and to come up with proposals for re-modelling the health and social care system in Ireland (north and south) and Scotland.

The issue of pensions would also have to be addressed as people in receipt of public sector pensions would need reassurance that they would not lose out following separation of Scotland and Northern Ireland from the United Kingdom. The attitude of the British government would be critical here and the meeting noted that the Alliance would need to put pressure on the Johnson administration throughout 2022 to ensure a satisfactory outcome on this key issue.

Cross-border trade was an issue likely to be of concern mainly to voters in Scotland and the Alliance would need to liaise with sympathetic contacts in the European Commission to see what meat might be put on the bones of earlier predictions that the accession arrangements for the Gaelic Federation could include special measures to mitigate possible disruption on the border between Scotland and England.

Finally, it was agreed that the issue of cross-community conflict in Northern Ireland could be dealt with effectively by the very concept of the Gaelic Federation. Continuing links with Scotland and the balanced religious makeup of the Federation would hopefully act to reassure loyalists.

The meeting closed with agreement to hold the next AGM in January 2023, to enable an analysis to be carried out on the results of the expected December polls and a follow-on plan to be developed for the ensuing year. The meeting would be held in Dublin.

*****

The GA secretariat now turned their attention to the preparation of the information document to be issued in advance of the December 2022 polls. Jim Kearney volunteered to lead on the drafting and to share drafts with Mary Douglas and Sean Donnelly at key points in the process.

An initial run through the issues that would need to be addressed suggested that a good level of reassurance could be given on most of them, with the exception of the position regarding public sector pensions. As things stood, it would be impossible to include in the document a guarantee that the British government would honour its pension commitments to civil servants and other public sector workers in Scotland and Northern Ireland after their withdrawal from the United Kingdom. It was agreed that Jane Harrington and John Campbell should be asked to begin political lobbying on this issue.

Jim also agreed to get in touch with Niall Murphy to see if it would be possible to get a firmer commitment on the earlier informal indications that the Commission would probably put in place a special package to ease the accession to the EU of the Gaelic Federation and to mitigate potential economic problems around the new international Scottish-English border.

Drafting got under way in early February, starting with the issues that had already been teased out in earlier deliberations. On the general issue of the economy, leaving aside specific border issues, reliance would be placed on the performance of the EU economies in general and the Irish economy in particular, when compared to the sluggish British economy. The paper would detail all the key economic indicators and conclude that, for Scotland and Northern Ireland, there was nothing to lose and everything to gain from leaving the UK and re-joining the EU in partnership with Ireland. The paper would also need to re-assure voters in the Irish Republic that, freed from the drag of the under-performing UK economy, Scotland and Northern Ireland would be likely to provide a boost to, rather than a drag on, Ireland's performance within the European Union. Any assurances that might be forthcoming from the Commission on special funding, linked to the accession arrangements, would clearly be helpful in this respect.

To the extent that Irish voters might, nevertheless, perceive a degree of risk in committing to the Federation, this would be significantly offset by explaining the advantages of the new constitution for cross-community relations. Bearing in mind the spill over effect on life in the Republic over the 30 years of the Troubles, Irish voters would be likely to be attracted by any development that finally dealt with the root causes of inter-community conflict. This section of the paper would be particularly important for the loyalist community in Northern Ireland in that it would address several of their objections to secession from the United Kingdom. In particular, it would retain the link with Scotland, the part of the UK to which loyalists had the greatest affinity, and it would ensure that the religious make-up of the new political entity would be broadly balanced, unlike the situation in a free-standing United Ireland.

Scottish voters' concerns about the currency to be used in an independent Scotland could be assuaged by pointing to the benefits Ireland had enjoyed through its involvement in the euro. The country's rapid recovery from the 2008 economic crash was in no small measure due to its participation in the single currency. Any fears Scots might have had about having to adopt the euro as a freestanding, independent Scotland could be mitigated by the thought that, through the Federation, they would be embarking on this journey in partnership with a country that was already using the euro successfully.

By mid-May, Jim had produced the first draft of the sections dealing with general aspects of the economy, currency issues and avoiding community conflict. The question of pensions would have to await the results of lobbying by the GA presidents and the line to take on Scottish border issues was dependent on feedback from Niall Murphy. Jim circulated his partial draft to Sean Donnelly and Mary Douglas and turned his attention to the other big outstanding issue – healthcare.

*****

Jane Harrington and John Campbell had been working hard, lobbying the British government on the issue of public sector pensions. They had had limited success. The responses they were getting were very evasive, with the general line being that this was a hypothetical matter that could be addressed if and when it became a real issue. They would not be drawn on the parallel of pension cover for British civil servants who had been working for the European Commission prior to Brexit. This had been conceded, albeit reluctantly, as part of the financial settlement in the Withdrawal Agreement. Why then could the same principle not be conceded for Scottish and Northern Irish civil servants who would have earned their pensions working in the UK civil service prior to Scottish and Northern Irish independence? It was to no avail; the government would not be drawn.

To be fair, the government did have its hands pretty full dealing with multiple problems in the economy, not least the vexed question of agreeing trade deals to replace those lost through departure from the European Union. Following the government's back down on the holding of the Scottish Independence referendum and the Irish border poll, a deal had finally been concluded with the United States, but this fell far short of the level of trade needed to compensate for the flimsy deal with the EU.

The reality of Brexit was creating particular problems for Northern Ireland. The Irish border protocol in the Withdrawal Agreement provided for Northern Ireland to remain close to the EU single market and customs union and, contrary to the oft-repeated assertions of Boris Johnson that this would not require any sort of border in the Irish Sea, Northern Ireland was now having to implement a range of controls on goods entering the province from Great Britain.

Although goods destined for Northern Ireland were not subject to regulatory controls, checks and controls were nevertheless necessary in view of the possibility of goods moving over the Irish border into the EU. The necessary controls were proving expensive and were leading to significant price increases on British goods sold in the province. Quite a few British companies were responding to the situation by ceasing trading in Northern Ireland altogether, resulting in non-availability of a range of products.

At a macro-economic level, Northern Ireland was actually faring well, as the province had continuing free access for its goods to both the EU single market and the British market. The issue of higher prices for British goods and non-availability of some products would be dealt with in time by progressive substitution of trade from the EU for trade from Great Britain. This was not of course a narrative that appealed to the DUP. Having played a significant part in delivering Brexit, they were now crying foul about the consequences of their anti-EU stance. Efforts by the EU to mitigate problems at a technical level did not impress the DUP as their principal objection to the Protocol was a political one linked to a perceived weakening of the link to Great Britain.

By now, the realisation had dawned on Boris Johnson's government that the UK's 31 December departure from the European Union with a minimalist trade deal had been a mistake. It had always been the view of informed commentators that a comprehensive deal would be necessary sooner or later, but this was now becoming clear even to the Tories. Moves were afoot to start fresh trade talks between the United Kingdom and the European Union but the difference this time around was that the UK would be negotiating as a Third Country, not as a departing member of the EU club. Threats to undermine the Northern Ireland Protocol by invoking Article 16 had been dropped as it was clear such a move would result in setting aside the existing minimalist trade deal, never mind the prospect of new talks to improve the deal.

When the talks did finally get going, the atmosphere was very different from that which had prevailed in the latter stages of the Transition Phase. The UK's position was considerably weaker and the EU was moving on economically. There was no sign of the bellicose language that had characterised the UK's approach in earlier discussions.

Jim Kearney was keeping abreast of these developments. He had a report back from Jane Harrington about the Government's reluctance to discuss the pension issue and wondered if there might be an opportunity here to put some pressure on the Tories to address the matter. Jim made contact with Niall Murphy, explained the position and asked for his advice. As Niall was responsible for preparing negotiating briefs for the EU negotiator, there was a clear path through to the talks. Niall felt there was a good chance that the Commission would be sympathetic, given their strong support for the concept of a Gaelic Federation within the European Union. He promised to raise it with the team. He would also discuss the question of what sort of accession package might be available in the event of the Federation getting the go-ahead at the December polls.

With these two issues on the back burner for the time being, Jim continued with his drafting of the health section of the GA information document.

The National Health Service in the UK had achieved almost iconic status over the years and it would be a very brave politician who would even hint at the idea of changing it. The performance of the NHS during the peak of the Covid-19 pandemic in 2020 had received mixed reviews. On the one hand, the staff of the NHS had been hailed as heroes and had been loudly applauded by the whole population on successive Thursday evenings throughout the worst of the first lockdown. On the other hand, many failings had been exposed, including lack of stockpiles of PPE (Personal Protective Equipment) for front line staff, shortage of intensive care beds and ventilators and slowness in getting up to speed with testing for the virus. These problems had their origins in the years of austerity under the Tory government elected in 2015.

It was difficult to work out where the mood of the public lay. Post-Covid, would the consensus be that the NHS, as currently constituted, was sacrosanct or would the failings that had been exposed point to the need for some level of reform? How would people in Northern Ireland react to the prospect of aligning with the health service in the Republic? To be sure, consumers in the Republic had indicated a high level of satisfaction with the services they were receiving. A survey commissioned in 2007 found that patient satisfaction was high with 90% of inpatients and 85% of outpatients indicating that they were satisfied with the services they received but there was some evidence that satisfaction levels had declined in recent years. People in Northern Ireland were used to the concept of free healthcare 'from the cradle to the grave' and the idea of having to pay part of the cost of healthcare directly to the provider was unlikely to prove attractive.

Jim concluded that there would be merit in studying the healthcare systems operating in other countries in Europe to see if there might be a system that would cap both the British and the Irish systems in terms of quality of care and value for money. Having looked at services operating in a range of countries, he came to the conclusion that France offered the best model to inform a new and improved system for the Gaelic Federation. He found that the French health care system was generally recognised as offering one of the best services in the world. It was acknowledged to be a system that worked, that provided universal coverage and that was strongly defended by virtually everyone in France.

His research showed that the French system was funded in part by obligatory health contributions levied on all salaries and paid by employers, employees and the self-employed, in part by central government funding, and in part by users who normally had to pay a small fraction of the cost of most health care interventions they received. In European terms, the French system was among the better funded as far as share of GDP was concerned and indicators like numbers of GPs, nursing professionals and hospital beds compared favourably with other EU countries. Compared specifically to the UK, funding and number of GPs were 10% higher while there were more than twice as many hospital beds and more than 40% more nurses and midwives than in the UK.

Jim decided to include in the draft Information Document a policy for the Gaelic Federation of moving in the direction of the French health care system. He would include comparative costings and contribution rates as between the current NHS system, the current RoI system and the proposed French-style system. There was a risk that people in Northern Ireland and Scotland would baulk at the idea of having to contribute to the cost of their healthcare but the document would point out that they were already paying for NHS care through National Insurance contributions. It would also point out that, leaving aside relative performance on vaccination roll out where special factors applied, the higher level of funding enjoyed by the system in France had enabled the country to respond more effectively to the Covid-19 pandemic than the UK's underfunded system. It seemed likely that voters would accord a high priority to pandemic readiness with memories of the Covid nightmare still fresh in their memories.

The draft section on healthcare was duly circulated to Mary Douglas and Sean Donnelly for comment.

In early June, Jim heard back from Niall Murphy about the outcome of his discussions with the Commission on the prospects for an accession package to ease the re-entry of Scotland and Northern Ireland to the European Union and on the vexed question of pensions. Niall reported that the Commission were becoming increasingly frustrated with the attitude of the UK government to the new trade negotiations and were in no mood to offer concessions. On the contrary, they were inclined to introduce some red lines of their own to balance those that continued to be trotted out by the British side.

The good news was that the EU side would be happy to introduce a caveat related to the issue of pensions liability.

The Commission did not want to see the prospects for the Gaelic Federation dashed because of fears among pensioners about their future livelihoods. In the absence of a commitment from the British government to honour their liability in respect of Scottish and Northern Irish pensioners, there would be no progress with the new trade talks.

The news was not so good in relation to the details of an accession package to deal with the economic consequences of secession. Niall had been told it would be factually correct to allude to the probability of such a package, given that countries acceding to the EU did generally benefit from such packages. In advance of the political decision to secede, however, it would not be possible to specify authoritatively the nature and content of such a package. The Alliance would, nevertheless, be free to speculate and could do so effectively by alluding to what had happened in past examples of accession.

Armed with this new information, and on the assumption that the British government would soon give way on the pensions issue, Jim Kearney was now in a position to finalise drafting of the GA information document, which he accomplished by early July. The completed draft was now circulated to all members of the GA Executive Committee with a target of agreeing the final shape of the document by the end of July.

Meanwhile, political parties generally were gearing up for the December polls and were preparing their own policy documents relating to the vote. The parties in Scotland and Northern Ireland were dividing into three camps – those who supported the status quo, those supporting Scottish independence or a United Ireland and those supporting the proposed Gaelic Federation. In the Irish Republic, there was minority support for the status quo with roughly equal support for the other two options.

With less than six months to go to the December independence and border polls, politicians turned their attention to the parameters for the two referenda and the questions that should be asked. A working group of key representatives of the British, Scottish, Irish and Northern Irish governments was established and, after two weeks of discussions and debate, came up with the following agreement:

1. All registered voters in Scotland over the age of 16 would be eligible to vote in the Scottish independence referendum.
2. All registered voters in Ireland and Northern Ireland over the age of 16 would be eligible to vote in the Irish border poll.
3. A simple majority of votes cast would be sufficient to determine the outcome in both cases i.e., there would be no thresholds.
4. In the Irish border poll there would also be a requirement for a majority in both jurisdictions.
5. A vote for an independent Scotland would be accepted as binding.
6. A vote for a United Ireland would be accepted as binding.
7. A vote for a Gaelic Federation would be regarded as advisory and would need to be confirmed by parliamentary votes in the new Scottish and all-Ireland legislatures.

8. The voting would take place on Thursday 8 December.

The questions to be asked in the referenda would be as follows:

Irish Border Poll

1. Please select your preferred option by placing an X in the appropriate box:
   o I would prefer to retain the existing constitutional arrangements.
   o I would prefer a union between Northern Ireland and the Republic of Ireland.
2. If you voted for a union between Northern Ireland and the Republic of Ireland, please indicate the context in which you would like this to happen by placing an X in the appropriate box:
   o I would prefer a freestanding United Ireland.
   o I would prefer a union between Northern Ireland and the Republic of Ireland within the framework of a constitutional federation with Scotland.

Scottish Independence Referendum

1. Please select your preferred option by placing an X in the appropriate box.
   o I would prefer to retain the existing constitutional arrangements.
   o I would prefer an independent Scotland.

2. If you voted for an Independent Scotland, please indicate the context in which you would like this to happen by placing an X in the appropriate box:
   o I would prefer a freestanding independent Scotland.
   o I would prefer an independent Scotland within the framework of a constitutional federation with Ireland.

The executive committee of the Gaelic Alliance had lobbied hard for the Gaelic Federation option to be binding but accepted the logic of the decision to require an additional parliamentary process for union between Scotland and Ireland. In the event that the status quo was rejected and the federation option achieved a bigger percentage referendum vote than the freestanding independence option, it seemed unlikely that the new Scottish and Irish parliaments would proceed to vote in the opposite direction. Much would depend on the make-up of the legislatures resulting from the elections to the new parliaments and it would be important for the Gaelic Alliance to work hard to maximise the pro-federation vote in those elections.

In September, following the summer vacation, the political parties ramped up their activity levels and began campaigning in earnest for their preferred outcomes at the December polls. Pushing for the status quo were the DUP in Northern Ireland, the Scottish Conservative Party (with support from the UK government), half of Scottish Labour and a proportion of the Lib Dems (both parties had allowed a free vote). Arguing for freestanding independence were a proportion of the SNP (again a free vote on the issue of the

Federation had been allowed), Fianna Fail in Ireland and the majority of Sinn Fein. The remainder of the SNP, Scottish Labour and Scottish Lib Dems, Fine Gael and Labour in the Republic, a minority of Sinn Fein plus Alliance and SDLP in Northern Ireland were backing the Gaelic Federation. In all three jurisdictions, the Greens were supporting the Gaelic Federation.

Information documents had been prepared by all the groupings to assist voters in deciding which way to cast their votes. The draft GA document prepared by Jim Kearney had been approved by the other members of the Executive Committee and would be ready to launch once the issue of public sector pensions had been resolved. Fortunately, in early October, the trade negotiations between the UK and the EU produced the result the Alliance had been hoping for – in order to unblock progress, the British negotiating team conceded that the UK government would be obliged to honour its pension commitments to Scottish and Northern Irish public sector employees and the trade talks were able to continue.

Following the launch of the information documents, there was a flurry of activity on all the main media platforms. Jane Harrington, Maeve McDermott and John Campbell were in great demand and were very effective in coordinating the campaign on behalf of the pro-federation parties. The status quo campaign and the campaign favouring freestanding independence for Scotland and Ireland struggled to match the enthusiasm of the pro-federation lobby. As the 8 December referendum date approached, opinion polls all pointed to the likelihood of a resounding victory for the federation option.

And so, it transpired. Voting on 8 December was hot and heavy from the off and exit polls that evening deviated only slightly from the opinion poll predictions. By 2:00 am on 9 December, it was clear that Scotland and Northern Ireland were set to leave the United Kingdom and that a significant majority of those voting for separation were also in favour of the federation option.

The final results of the polls were as follows:

Scotland
For the status quo – 41%
For an independent Scotland – 59%
For a Gaelic Federation – 62% of the 59%

Northern Ireland
For the status quo – 39%
For a United Ireland 61%
For a Gaelic Federation – 69% of the 61%

Republic of Ireland
For the status quo – 25%
For a United Ireland – 75%
For a Gaelic Federation – 59% of the 75%

Jim Kearney and his colleagues couldn't have hoped for a better result. Efforts would have to be re-doubled in the New Year to ensure that the support for the Gaelic Federation was maintained as independent Scotland and re-united Ireland emerged into the brave new world of 2023. But for now, there was partying to be done!

Waterfront Hall, Belfast – venue for the Gaelic Alliance AGM on
27 January 2022
(Copyright William Murphy: Creative Commons Attribution –
ShareAlike 2.0 Generic (CC-BY-SA-2.0))

Boris Johnson assured the people of Northern Ireland there would
be no border in the Irish Sea, post-Brexit
(Creative Commons Attribution – ShareAlike 4.0 International
(CC-BY-SA-4.0))

The England-Scotland border:
a key issue for the Gaelic Alliance
(Copyright Taras Young: Creative Commons Attribution –
ShareAlike 4.0 International (CC-BY-SA-4.0))

An illustration of the high regard for the NHS
(© Copyright Bill Nicholls: Creative Commons Attribution –
ShareAlike 2.0 Generic (CC-BY-SA-2.0))

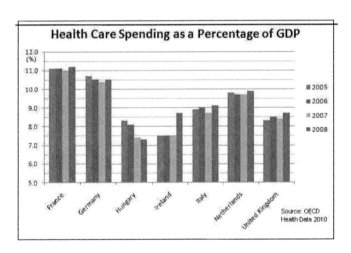

France and the UK at opposite ends of the range of health care
spending in Europe

Chapter 10
The Gaelic Federation

The 2022 AGM of the Gaelic Alliance was held at Trinity College, Dublin on Thursday 12 January 2023. Following the incredible results of the Scottish independence and Irish border polls, the mood was jubilant. The Executive Committee was praised for their work in delivering so emphatically on the Alliance's objectives and all the office bearers were returned unopposed for another year.

The meeting turned to the main business of the day – the analysis of the referendum results and planning for GA activity in the year ahead. Although it seemed inconceivable that the parliaments in Edinburgh and Dublin, due to be returned in May, would fail to follow through on voters' expressed preference for independence linked to a federation of the two new nations, many delegates expressed concern that the prize could still be lost if the momentum they had built up in 2022 wasn't maintained.

Various ideas were floated for keeping the federation objective fresh in people's minds. Another march in the lead up to the general elections, expected to be in May, would be helpful, and in the preceding weeks, party political broadcasts and media interviews would be exploited to keep the message centre stage. There was still a concern amongst a proportion of delegates that the political parties who had supported the federation concept at the referendum stage, either whole-heartedly by making it party policy or partly through allowing a free vote, might begin to weaken their resolve in the months leading up to the elections.

Following several hours of debate on this issue, an idea emerged which began to gather more and more support. The idea was for the Alliance to change its status from a campaigning organisation to a fully-fledged political party. This would allow a more direct appeal to the electorates rather than having to work through existing political parties. It would still be important to keep those parties on board but this might be easier to achieve from a position of increased political strength. If a sufficient number of candidates willing to put their names forward could be found from amongst the Alliance's huge membership, the Alliance would be entitled to its own party-political broadcasts, again facilitating a more direct appeal to the public.

A motion was put to the meeting, calling for the creation of a Gaelic Alliance Party, and was passed with an overwhelming majority. The meeting then moved swiftly on to consider the issue of party leadership. In view of the success of the three national presidents in convincing voters to opt for the federation option in the referenda, it was decided that the leader should be chosen from amongst these three. A ballot was held and Jane Harrington emerged as the successful candidate.

Jim Kearney and his colleagues on the secretariat were given the job of following through on the legal processes required for changing the status of the organisation, with a target of having the new party up and running by the end of

February. They would also start planning for the various media interventions that had been approved by the delegates on the understanding that implementation of these did not need to await the formal establishment of the party. The Alliance would start campaigning straight away and would use the impending status change of the organisation as an additional hook on which to hang its publicity campaign.

*****

The New Year had got off to a stormy start at Westminster. Tory back benchers were rebelling on a range of issues, including: the government's failure to deliver on the levelling up of economic investment in northern constituencies, dislocation of trade with the EU due to divergence of rules and consequent re-imposition of tariffs and rules-of origin disputes affecting sales of British cars in the EU and problems over declining animal welfare standards linked to imports under the trade deal with the USA. Added to the mix, there was now the need to process legislation to give effect to the decision of Scotland and Northern Ireland to leave the United Kingdom. The only silver lining for Boris Johnson's beleaguered government was the prospect of a bigger Tory majority following the departure of the troublesome Remainer nations!

The Tories' comfortable 80-seat majority following the December 2019 general election had been whittled away to 63 as a result of a series of disastrous bye-election defeats to the rejuvenated Labour Party.

On occasions the government's majority was reduced to uncomfortable levels through rebel Tory MPs voting with the opposition. However, following the departure of MPs from Scotland and Northern Ireland, the government's majority would go up to a more comfortable level. This could have been one of the reasons for the reasonably smooth passage through parliament of the bill providing for Scottish and Northern Irish secession. The bill had passed all its stages in both houses by the middle of March, and the way was now clear for elections to the new parliaments in Scotland and Ireland to take place on 11 May. The constituencies would be those already identified for Dail elections in the Republic, Assembly elections in Northern Ireland and Parliamentary elections in Scotland.

In the meantime, the GA secretariat was working on the procedures for establishing the Gaelic Alliance Party. In the end, the process was more straightforward than expected and the party was up and running by the third week in February. Work had also been proceeding on the identification of candidates to contest the May elections. Following the AGM, a circular had been sent to all 180,000 members and such was the response that each seat could have been filled three times over. Selection committees, established in each constituency, were given the job of identifying the best candidates – 129 were needed in Scotland, 90 in the former Northern Ireland and 160 in the former Republic of Ireland. The work of the selection committees had been completed by the first week of March and the party was ready to start serious campaigning for the May elections.

*****

Soon after the referendum results in Scotland and Ireland, a special committee had been established, comprising representatives of the UK and Irish governments and the devolved administrations in Scotland and Northern Ireland. This committee had been given the job of advising on the new parliamentary structures and associated election arrangements to apply following the enactment of the secession bill.

Early on in its proceedings, this committee reached the conclusion that, so as not to delay the process unduly, existing arrangements should be disturbed as little as possible. To the extent that this would produce less-than-ideal constitutional arrangements, the new governments in Dublin and Edinburgh would be able to introduce changes over time to produce an optimal system. In any case, these arrangements would be very different, depending on whether the final decision was to maintain two free-standing nations or to endorse the concept of a Gaelic Federation.

The key points agreed were as follows:

- Scotland would continue to elect 129 MPs, with 73 being elected on the first past the post system and 56 by the additional member PR system.
- Ireland would elect 250 TDs (160 from 39 constituencies in the former Republic and 90 from 18 constituencies in the former Northern Ireland).
- The single transferrable vote PR system which had applied in Northern Ireland and the Republic, would continue to be used.
- The Irish Seanad would cease to exist with the dissolution of the Dail and the new parliament would decide on what, if anything, should replace it.

The elections were just two months away and all the parties in Scotland and Ireland had their campaigns in full swing. There was a great buzz in both countries, in stark contrast to the situation in England and Wales.

The sunny uplands promised by the Leave campaign had yet to materialise and every week seemed to bring more depressing economic news. Relocations of car manufacturers and other large employers to European Union countries were continuing apace and the unemployment rate was rocketing. Efforts to negotiate an improved trade agreement with the EU had been bogged down for months and the additional trade resulting from the deal with the US was proving to be a poor substitute for that lost through dislocation with Europe. This situation was not playing well with the public and Kier Starmer's Labour Party was building up an impressive lead over the Tories in the opinion polls. Boris Johnson faced a Herculean task if he was to reverse his party's fortunes before the May 2024 general election.

Meanwhile, the May 2023 elections in Scotland and Ireland were just around the corner. The Gaelic Alliance Party was moving up in the polls, as were all the parties favouring the federation option. Jane Harrington was performing well as GAP Leader and had appointed an impressive group of the party's election candidates to act as spokespersons in different policy areas in each jurisdiction. John Campbell had been appointed leader-in-waiting for Scotland and Maeve McDermott would be Jane's deputy in Ireland. All were getting significant media exposure and, so far, no skeletons had emerged from anybody's cupboard. A number of party-political broadcasts had been aired and those from the Alliance seemed to have gone down particularly well with the electorate. The party had also organised marches in Dublin and Edinburgh which had attracted huge media interest and generated mostly positive reaction.

*****

Election day in Scotland and Ireland, 11 May, dawned bright and sunny and business at the polling stations in both countries was brisk from the start. Based on exit polling, it became clear, as the 10:00 pm deadline for voting approached, that those supporting the federation option had done well. As polls closed, there was optimism in the air over GAP headquarters in Belfast.

That optimism had been well founded. The final Scottish results were announced on 14 May and the Irish results were finalised two days later, due to the vagaries of the single transferable voting system. The Gaelic Alliance Party received 42% of the popular vote in Scotland and 47% in Ireland. Together with other federation-supporting parties and groups, it seemed that Jane Harrington's party would have little difficulty in forming a majority government in both Edinburgh and Dublin. The party's fears that some of the support from other parties might have weakened in the time since the referenda, turned out to be unfounded. The size of the GAP lead over other parties had probably played a part in solidifying that support.

As might have been expected, when both parliaments got going, the first significant business of the day, following the election of speakers and the advancing of other procedural business, was the process to be followed to give effect to the expressed wish of the electorates for a federation of the two nations. Many of those who had voted for Scottish independence and for a United Ireland had done so in the context of the proposed federation and going back on this was hardly an option. The mood of both parliaments was strongly behind this conclusion and lively debates ensued as to the best way to proceed.

The two governments kept in close touch as the debates continued and successfully steered proceedings towards an agreed outcome. The decision was to appoint a joint commission of the two parliaments with a remit to consider all legalities and practicalities associated with the federation concept and to come up with a blueprint for implementation. The Commission would have one year in which to carry out its work and submit its report. Some of the ideas that had attracted support during the parliamentary debates would be made available to the Commission to include in its deliberations. These included the idea of locating the federal parliament at Parliament Buildings, Stormont and the idea of adopting a federation flag based on a combination of the crosses of St Andrew and St Patrick.

Pending receipt of the Commission's report in June 2024, Ireland and Scotland would still need to be governed and so the two governments got down to business at the level of their individual nations. An important piece of that business would relate to the European Union. As things stood, part of Ireland already had full EU membership, the other part of Ireland had a close association through the famous Protocol and Scotland was, as yet, a Third Country.

It was agreed that the Irish Minister of State for European Affairs, supported by the Scottish Minister for

Foreign Affairs should open up exploratory talks with the European Commission to agree the process for progressing the accession of the Federation. In due course, this would become a federal level responsibility, but it would be some time before the relevant federal minister would be in post and it made sense to advance matters as far as possible in the meantime. The Commission had already indicated that they would be happy to proceed on this basis.

Parliament Buildings, Stormont
(Copyright © Brian Shaw: Creative Commons Attribution –
ShareAlike 2.0 Generic (CC-BY-SA-2.0))

The debating chamber, Stormont
(Copyright © Stephen McKay: Creative Commons Attribution –
ShareAlike 2.0 Generic (CC-BY-SA-2.0))

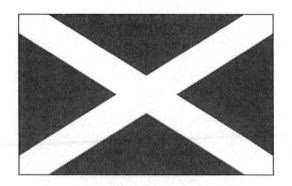

Cross of St Andrew

+

Cross of St Patrick

=

Flag of the Gaelic Federation?

Chapter 11
The Death Throes of Brexit

In the early months of 2024, a series of opinion polls showed an ever-increasing lead for the Labour Party over the Conservatives. More detailed questions in the polls revealed that the most important issue driving voters away from Boris Johnson's government was – believe it or not – Brexit! People had finally woken up to the fact that leaving the European Union had not been a smart move. The country was on its uppers economically and most people were in no doubt where the blame lay.

The government had made a valiant attempt to blame Covid-19 for the severe economic downturn and indeed many commentators had predicted that this would be their approach. Fortunately, people in England and Wales were now wise to this sort of trickery; they had noticed that the economies of a number of EU member states, including Ireland, were recovering quite well and they quickly rejected the government's claim. They had been taken in by spurious arguments in the lead up to Brexit and the period leading to the UK's actual departure. They were not going to fall for it again.

The Labour Party was not slow to read the situation and, following some internal debate, announced its new policy on

Europe in the first week of March. They would now campaign strongly for the re-entry of England and Wales to the European Union. It had been clear from the comments of several European leaders and senior eurocrats that a reversal of Brexit would be welcomed, albeit that the favourable terms previously enjoyed by the United Kingdom would no longer be available.

This move by the Labour Party had the effect of further increasing their lead in the polls and it was no surprise when, on 2 May, the Tories crashed to a resounding defeat. Labour came in with an overall majority of 56 seats.

One month later, the commission set up by the Irish and Scottish governments to produce a blueprint for the Gaelic Federation delivered its report. The key recommendations were:

- The Federal Parliament should be located at Parliament Buildings, Stormont.
- Powers reserved to the Federal Parliament should comprise foreign policy, defence and taxation.
- Other matters should be dealt with by the national legislatures in Dublin and Edinburgh.
- Elections to the Federal Parliament should be by Proportional Representation (PR) using the single transferable vote system.
- There should be 120 MPs at federal level – 56 from Scotland (4 from each of 14 constituencies), 16 from the former Northern Ireland (4 from each of 4 constituencies) and 48 from the former Republic of Ireland (4 from each of 12 constituencies).

- These new constituencies should be formed by appropriate redrawing of the boundaries of the existing 73 first-past-the post constituencies in Scotland, the existing 18 PR constituencies in Northern Ireland and the existing 39 PR constituencies in the Republic of Ireland.
- The number of MPs returned to the Scottish Parliament should remain unchanged at 129.
- The number of TDs returned to the Irish Parliament should remain unchanged at 250 (90 from the former Northern Ireland and 160 from the former Republic of Ireland).
- The leader of the party gaining most votes at the federal election should be designated President and head of state of the Federation, with the leaders of the parties gaining most votes at the national elections being designated Prime Minister.
- Before the elections in 2029, consideration should be given to conducting a review of constituency boundaries for the national elections leading to a reduction in the number of representatives returned to the two national parliaments.
- Scotland should move to proportional representation, using the single transferable vote system, in time for the 2029 elections.
- The flag of the Gaelic Federation should comprise an amalgamation of the crosses of St Patrick and St Andrew.

- Public buildings in Scotland should fly the St Andrew's saltire, the flag of the Gaelic Federation and the flag of the European Union.
- The Irish tricolour should be replaced by the St Patrick saltire.
- Public buildings in Ireland should fly the St Patrick saltire, the flag of the Gaelic Federation and the flag of the European Union.
- The Gaelic language (the Irish language/Scots Gallic) should be adopted as an official language of the Federation.
- A competition should be arranged for the composition of a new national anthem for the Federation. This might usefully reflect aspects of the traditional music of Ireland and Scotland.

The Commission's report was debated in both national parliaments over a period of several weeks. As is often the case in Ireland, the issue generating the most heat related to flags. A significant minority of TDs from constituencies of the former Republic of Ireland objected to the proposed change from the tricolour to the cross of St Patrick. They argued, not without logic, that the tricolour had itself been an exercise in reconciliation. The flag represented a truce (white) between the orange and green traditions. While this was historically correct, the tricolour had nevertheless come to be regarded by unionists as a symbol of republicanism and, as such, would be difficult for people from the former Northern Ireland to accept. After much heated debate, the St Patrick saltire was accepted as the flag of the New Ireland.

The other issue provoking considerable debate in both parliaments was the question of the new national anthem for the Federation. The idea of launching a competition for the composition of a suitable anthem did not find much favour and a joint committee of the two parliaments was commissioned to come up with an alternative suggestion. Their deliberations led to the proposal that Phil Coulter should be invited to compose the anthem. He had composed 'Ireland's Call', the anthem sung at international rugby matches (and now adopted as the anthem of the New Ireland), and it was felt that a Federation anthem in a similar genre would be appropriate. Flower of Scotland, the previously unofficial anthem of Scotland, had already been adopted as the official national anthem of independent Scotland.

Subject to these changes, it was agreed by both parliaments that the Commission's report should be accepted and that implementation of the recommendations should proceed. The aim would be to hold the first federal election on Friday, 21 March 2025.

*****

Kier Starmer's new government lost no time in getting down to business, and high on the agenda was the opening up of discussions in Brussels on the accession of the Kingdom of England and Wales to the European Union. Discussions with the joint negotiating team from Ireland and Scotland were already underway and the odd situation was now about to arise of two sets of negotiations running in parallel for the complicated reversal of Brexit.

The negotiations with Ireland and Scotland had been proceeding very smoothly. An aspect of accession to the European Union, which normally takes an inordinate amount of time, is the alignment of the new member state with the *acquis communautaire* – the accumulated legislation, legal acts and court decisions which constitute the body of EU law. As part of Ireland was already a member and Scotland and the other part of Ireland had until recently held membership as part of the United Kingdom, everything was already aligned.

The decision was taken early on that the Federation would join on the terms already enjoyed by the Republic of Ireland, including membership of the Eurozone. The one treaty that the Republic had opted out of was the Schengen Treaty. This treaty had established Europe's Schengen area, in which internal border checks had largely been abolished. It was signed on 14 June 1985, near the town of Schengen in Luxembourg by five of the ten member states of the then European Economic Community. Subsequently, Ireland had been unable to join Schengen because the UK was opposed and it would have been impossible to maintain the common travel area operating across the British Isles with one party in and the other out.

The European Commission held most of the trump cards in the negotiations with Kier Starmer's team, however, and there was a good prospect that both the Gaelic Federation and the Kingdom of England and Wales would end up in the Schengen Area.

The remaining outstanding issue in the EU/GA negotiations was the vexed question of the Scottish/English border. As it was still unclear how or when the negotiations with England and Wales would end, it was important to put in place some protections for the Scottish economy. True to the informal assurances they had given Niall Murphy back in 2022, an accession package was tabled, which included provision for a system of import levies and export restitutions aimed at smoothing out any disruptions arising from potentially different regimes operating either side of the border. In derogation from the rules of the single market, there was also provision for the Federation to offer state aid to industries threatened by unfair English competition. All of these measures were time limited – they would remain in place for a period of three years or until the accession of England and Wales, whichever came first.

The EU/GA negotiations were successfully completed by the end of September and, subject to confirmation by the federal government when elected; the Gaelic Federation became the provisional new 7th member state of the European Union (replacing the Republic of Ireland) on 15 October 2024.

*****

The negotiations with England and Wales were not proceeding quite as smoothly as those with Ireland and Scotland. The *acquis* was not a problem as there had not been enough time since Brexit for the former UK to deviate much from the body of EU law; but there were difficulties arising from the UK's attempt to re-acquire some of the opt-outs and special arrangements that had been enjoyed by the United Kingdom.

Labour's negotiating team was not ready to die in the ditch over some of the issues – notably the opt outs from the social chapter and the working hours directive – as they had not agreed with them in the first place – but they did fight strongly for others, especially retention of the Thatcher rebate, the Schengen opt out and the right to retain the pound sterling. The Commission played hardball, pointing out that agreement on these issues might have been possible if the decision to re-enter the Union had been taken while the UK was in transition. Now that the Kingdom of England and Wales was negotiating as a Third Country, the normal rules of accession would have to apply.

It took some months for this disagreement to play out as the government was coming under strong parliamentary pressure to stick to its guns. The rump of the Brexiteer brigade was still making its presence felt at Westminster, but they no longer had the numbers to call the tune. Finally, on 15 January 2025, Kier Starmer's team conceded defeat and agreed to re-enter the Union on the terms insisted upon by the Commission. The Kingdom of England and Wales became the 28th EU member state on 27 February 2025.

Brexit had been an expensive blunder, costing billions of pounds and creating deep divisions politically, socially and geographically. It could be argued that the political structures that had emerged from the Brexit process, and the subsequent breakup of the United Kingdom were more logical than what had gone before in that they were more aligned with the cultural fault lines of the British Isles, but the price paid to achieve that outcome had been high indeed.

Flag of Ireland

Flag of the Gaelic Federation

Flag of the European Union

Flags to be flown on official buildings in Ireland

Flag of Scotland

Flag of the Gaelic Federation

Flag of the European Union

Flags to be flown on official buildings in Scotland